GIANTS
FROM THE PAST

THE AGE OF MAMMALS

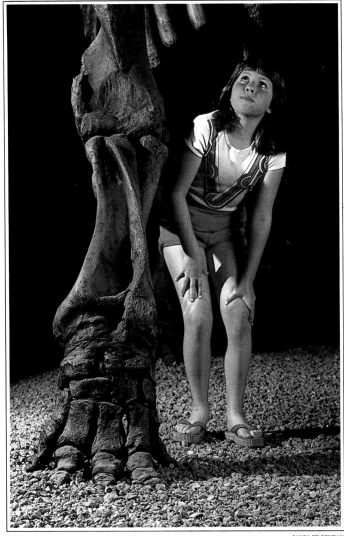

SANDY FELSENTHAL

PHOTOGRAPHS BY NATIONAL GEOGRAPHIC PHOTOGRAPHER

JOSEPH H. BAILEY

BOOKS FOR WORLD EXPLORERS
NATIONAL GEOGRAPHIC SOCIETY

CONTENTS

Copyright © 1983 National Geographic Society
Library of Congress CIP data: page 104

2

TITLE PAGE: A mastodon's leg bones amaze Heather Graham, 10, of Jackson, Michigan. The exhibit stands in the Illinois State Museum, in Springfield.

BELOW: Creatures of ten million years ago gather at a water hole on North America's plains. This scene greets visitors to the Smithsonian Institution's National Museum of Natural History, in Washington, D. C.

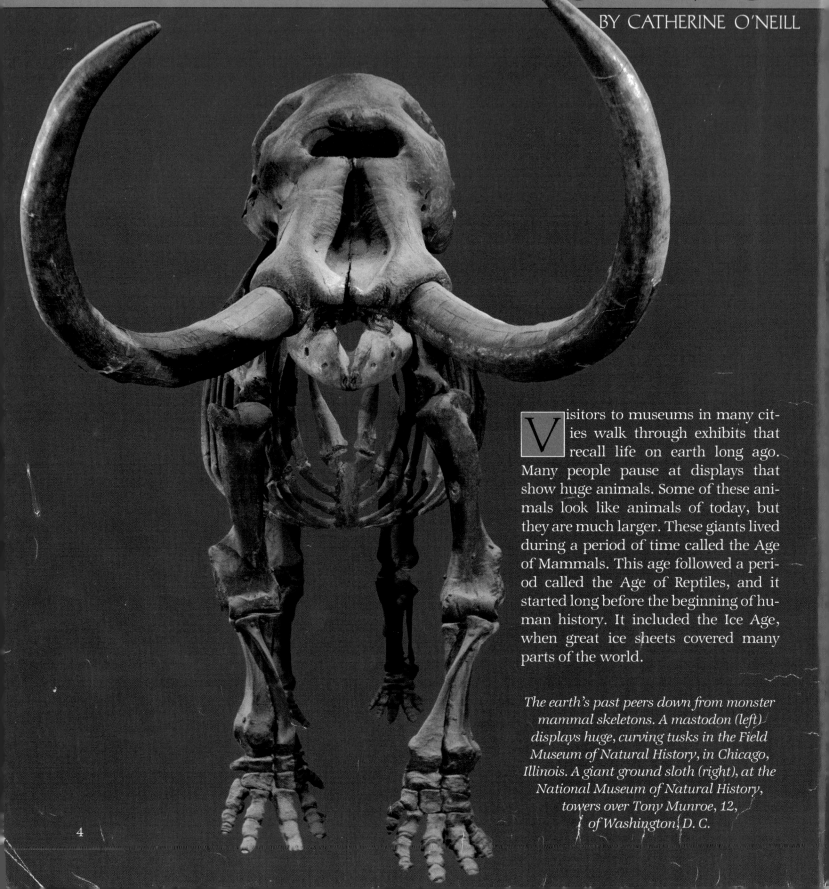

CHAPTER 1

SEARCH FOR GIANTS

BY CATHERINE O'NEILL

Visitors to museums in many cities walk through exhibits that recall life on earth long ago. Many people pause at displays that show huge animals. Some of these animals look like animals of today, but they are much larger. These giants lived during a period of time called the Age of Mammals. This age followed a period called the Age of Reptiles, and it started long before the beginning of human history. It included the Ice Age, when great ice sheets covered many parts of the world.

The earth's past peers down from monster mammal skeletons. A mastodon (left) displays huge, curving tusks in the Field Museum of Natural History, in Chicago, Illinois. A giant ground sloth (right), at the National Museum of Natural History, towers over Tony Munroe, 12, of Washington, D. C.

4

EARTH'S STORY

When you visit a museum of natural history, you see much more than human history. You see the history of the earth and the natural development of its animals and plants. Scientists learn about the earth's history by studying the remains of animals and plants. Where do they find these remains? Why, after thousands of years, are the remains still here?

Of the millions of animals that died, a few became buried in sand, mud, or even tar. In time, some of these materials turned into rock. The rock preserved the bones and other remains of the animals.

We call these remains fossils. A fossil can be a whole skeleton, a single bone, or a part of a bone. It can also be the print that a foot, a tree trunk, or a leaf made in the sand or mud.

You don't have to be a scientist to find a fossil. Children and adults on nature walks sometimes see them. Scientists called paleontologists (pay-lee-ahn-TAHL-uh-justs) make a lifetime study of fossils. By studying fossils, they learn what ancient animals looked like. They also learn what the animals ate, how large they were, and when they lived.

Much of paleontology is detective work. From clues left behind in the rocks, paleontologists have learned that mammals first appeared during the Age of Reptiles. Mammals are animals of all sizes that have some kind of hair, are warm-blooded, give birth to live young, and live on mother's milk when young. Reptiles are cold-blooded animals.

Present meets past as Washington, D. C., children visit the National Museum of Natural History. Elisa Arden, 9, and her brother Mark, 12, study a woolly mammoth skeleton. Woolly mammoths once roamed North America, protected from the Ice Age cold by their thick, shaggy coats. The animals stood more than 10 feet tall (3 m).* They used their long, curved tusks to scrape snow from plants.

*Metric figures in this book have been rounded off.

GIANTS OF THE ICE AGE

The Ice Age began two or three million years ago, scientists believe. Huge ice sheets covered large areas of the world. Then, after thousands of years, the ice sheets went away. Time after time the ice came and went. The animals shown here all lived during the Ice Age. Not all of them lived in one place. Beginning above and moving clockwise, the animals are: a saber-toothed cat, a giant Irish deer, an imperial mammoth, a giant beaver, and a giant camel. All lived in North America except for the Irish deer. It lived in Ireland and in many parts of Europe and Asia.

ROBERT E. HYNES

OTHER RESIDENTS OF EARTH

Certain reptiles, fish, and birds also grew amazingly large during the Age of Mammals. The giant tortoise, below, grew almost 5 feet long (2 m) and weighed as much as 800 pounds (363 kg). Its relatives still survive on remote islands in the Pacific and Indian Oceans. The giant shark, center, swam in ancient seas. It probably looked like a great white shark of today, but it was nearly twice as long—about 40 feet (12 m). The giant moa, right, a flightless bird, lived in New Zealand. It stood 11 feet tall (3 m).

ROBERT E. HYNES

In 1897, Dr. Erwin H. Barbour and his assistants (left) went on a fossil hunt in northwestern Nebraska. Fossil searches such as this gave Nebraska an early start in paleontology. Dr. Barbour stands second from the left.

Men who hunted for fossils of giant animals wore king-size boots on the 1897 dig (right). Other gear for this crew from the University of Nebraska State Museum included frying pans, a large coffee pot, and large-brimmed hats.

At Devil's Gulch, in north-central Nebraska (left), another crew from the museum displays its fossil finds of 1916. Millions of years ago, giant rhinoceroses and mastodons died here. Their bones became buried in the grasslands of North America.

FOSSIL HUNTING IN NEBRASKA

Paleontologists from the University of Nebraska State Museum found this huge mammoth skeleton near North Platte, Nebraska, in 1922. Mammoths were ancient animals related to elephants of today.

Nebraska is famous for its fossils. Museums and universities in many parts of the world display fossils from Nebraska. The state is very rich in bones of prehistoric mammals. Fossil remains include those of horses, rhinos, mammoths, saber-toothed cats, and ground sloths. Some of the bones are more than 30 million years old.

Fossil hunters have been digging up ancient bones in Nebraska for 150 years. Here you see some of these early diggers at work.

UNIVERSITY OF NEBRASKA STATE MUSEUM (ALL)

Dr. Barbour, in the dark suit, and other specialists assemble an imperial mammoth skeleton in 1933. It is the largest mounted mammoth skeleton in the world. It stands 14 feet tall (4 m) in the University of Nebraska State Museum, in Lincoln. The bones came from west-central Nebraska.

THE SEARCH GOES ON

All over the world, paleontologists continue the search for fossils. They hope the fossils will help them unlock secrets from the past. Finding certain fossils takes a lot of patience. Scientists spend days, or even weeks, walking over rocky areas. When they find bone chips or other evidence on the surface, they start digging. Many fossils are delicate. Scientists must carefully break apart the rocks to remove the fossils. When scientists make an important find, the careful work pays off. The men below helped hunt for fossils in northern Canada. They dug into a bank along the Old Crow River. There, they found bones of woolly mammoths, horses, giant beavers, and other animals. The remains had been preserved in material laid down by the river over a long time. Dr. Richard E. Morlan, of the National Museums of Canada, thinks some of the bones may be 165,000 years old.

KERBY SMITH

Student scientists gently dig up a mammoth tusk buried in a bank above the Old Crow River, in Canada's Yukon Territory (above). The tusk could be 165,000 years old. Some fossils found here show marks made by humans who carved bones into tools. Scientists think humans entered North America from Asia about 30,000 years ago.

14

This is how one fossil was formed. (1) A mammoth wades into a river to drink. (2) It dies near the bank. (3) Its bones lie there, partly covered by water and earth. (4) Each year the river rises and falls, sweeping away some of the bones and burying others. (5) Thousands of years pass. The river changes course from time to time. Finally, it cuts into the bank where a tusk and some bones remain. (6) The bank washes away, revealing the tusk.

PUZZLE OF THE PAST

Paleontologists keep their eyes open for even the tiniest bits of evidence. That's what Dr. Kathleen Smith was doing on the next-to-the-last day of a dig in Arizona. As she examined rocks, she noticed a fossil jawbone about as long as one of her fingernails.

The discovery of this bone was like finding a piece of a jigsaw puzzle. The more pieces you have, the easier it is to solve a puzzle.

The rock around the new find was at least 180 million years old. This told scientists the jaw was from an animal that lived during the Age of Reptiles. They already knew that the area of the dig had once been a swampy low-land. Dinosaur bones had been found there. So whatever the animal was, it lived in the same place—and at the same time—as dinosaurs.

Dr. Farish A. Jenkins, head of the expedition, knew immediately what kind of animal had been found. The shape of the teeth told him that it was a mammal and that it was an insect eater. The size of the jawbone told him the animal was about the size of a mouse. Since it was a mammal, it probably had fur. Most important, it lived long before the Age of Mammals began. Scientists think this animal, called a triconodont (try-CON-uh-dahnt), was one of the first mammals on earth.

One more piece of the puzzle of earth's past falls into place. Dr. Farish A. Jenkins, of Harvard University, headed the expedition that found this tiny jawbone (above, and circled at right) in Arizona's Painted Desert in 1981. It belonged to a mouse-size mammal that lived 180 million years ago, Dr. Jenkins says. Scientists know very little about the mammals of more than 65 million years ago. The Jenkins jawbone belonged to a kind of early mammal that was different from any other kinds that are now known.

Searching for fossils in the Arizona desert can be hot work (right). A scientific team works under a sunshade while digging up a fossil turtle. At one time green plants grew where these sun-baked rocks now lie. Before that, a part of the sea covered the desert.

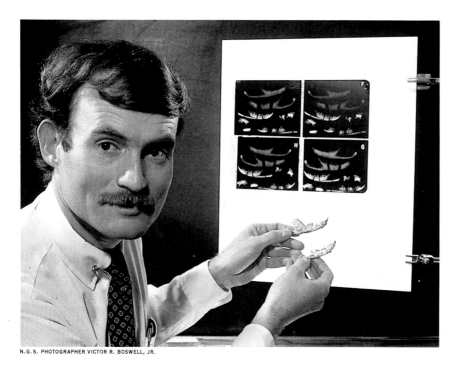

Dr. Jenkins holds lower jawbones from a kind of small mammal (left). It lived 80 million years later than the one whose jawbone appears on the opposite page. X-ray pictures on the wall behind him reveal details of teeth in upper and lower jawbones. Because teeth are harder than bone, they often last longer as fossils. By studying teeth and jaws, paleontologists can tell whether animals ate plants or meat. This kind was a meat eater. From other clues, Dr. Jenkins decided that this prehistoric mammal matched an opossum in size.

JAWS, JAWS, JAWS

Even icy Antarctica yields clues to the earth's past. Early in 1982, scientists discovered this piece of the jaw of a squirrel-size pouched mammal in Antarctica. It was the first fossil evidence that a forest-dwelling mammal once lived where neither forests nor land mammals exist today. The paper-clip-size fossil resembles others found in South America. Scientists agree that South America, Antarctica, and Australia were connected to each other millions of years ago. At that time, mammals could easily have migrated from one landmass to another.

Land bridges between continents provide travel routes for animals. As recently as 18,000 years ago, North America and Asia were joined by the Bering land bridge. Except for an ice-free pathway, the entire northern half of North America lay under the weight of the last great ice sheet. Animals had used the Bering land bridge many times before. Scientists believe that horses migrated westward across the bridge from America to Asia. Then they spread to Europe. People also think mammoths and mastodons moved east from Africa to North America by way of Asia. Other mammals headed south, crossing the Panamanian land bridge to South America. The giant sloth traveled across this bridge into North America.

GIANT LION   SABER-TOOTHED CAT

GLYPTODONT   GIANT BEAVER

GIANT SLOTH   HORSE   CAMEL

MAMMOTH   MASTODON

ASIA

BERING LAND BRIDGE

ICE SHEET

ICE SHEET

NORTH AMERICA

ATLANTIC OCEAN

SHORELINE 18,000 YEARS AGO

PACIFIC OCEAN

PANAMANIAN LAND BRIDGE

SOUTH AMERICA

ANIMALS AGAINST THE ICE

People have found fossils of early mammals all over the world. In ancient times, some kinds of animals that now live only in Asia or Africa roamed North America. How did they get from one continent to another? Did they all move at once? Did some remain behind and later die out?

Scientists continue to search for answers to these questions. They now think that the climate of the world and the shape of the land have changed greatly over millions of years. Water levels rose, and then fell. Landmasses appeared and disappeared.

Changes in the land affected the animals that lived on it. Over the last two or three million years, the earth went through a series of temperature shifts. This period is called the Pleistocene (PLY-stuh-seen) epoch. It is also called the Ice Age.

During the Pleistocene epoch, temperatures cooled and then warmed over and over again. Many theories, or ideas, explain why the ice came and went. Some scientists think there have been changes in the earth's orbit around the sun. Also, they believe that whole continents have moved. When such things happen, the climate changes.

During the cool periods, ice sheets covered huge areas. The level of the sea dropped because so much of the earth's water was locked up in ice. New land appeared—land once covered by water. In some places, the new land formed bridges between continents.

During warm periods, the ice sheets melted. The level of the ocean rose. Some of the land bridges disappeared. Animals that once had crossed such bridges couldn't return to their original homes.

With each climate change, the plants of the world also changed. Animals changed, too. Some found new places to live. Others developed bodies better suited to the new foods and living conditions. Some kinds did not change enough to survive. In time, they disappeared.

65 MILLION YEARS AGO

Scientists who study the earth believe that all the continents of today were once joined together. Over millions of years, they have slowly moved apart. They might have looked like this 65 million years ago. Movement deep below the surface of the earth causes the continents to move. How does this affect animals? When continents break apart, animals cannot travel from one to another. Animals left on each continent stay there and develop in differing ways.

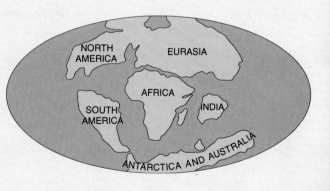

 PATRICIA K. CANTLAY, N.G.S. STAFF (ALL)

TOO SMALL FOR DINNER

When dinosaurs ruled the earth, tiny mammals began to appear. This painting shows how the world might have looked 75 or 80 million years ago. The toothy Tyrannosaurus (tih-ran-uh-SAWR-us) seems to be eyeing two mouse-size mammals for dinner, but they probably were more in danger of being stepped on than of being eaten. The horned Triceratops (try-SER-uh-tops) presented a little less danger because it was not a meat eater. Several million years later, as dinosaurs disappeared, the Age of Mammals began. Mammals of all sizes ruled the earth.

ROBERT E. HYNES

PARADE OF THE GIANTS

Dinosaurs disappeared 65 million years ago, and an amazing variety of mammals appeared in their place. The areas where dinosaurs had lived gradually changed, and so did the kinds of animals that lived there. Swampy lowlands became grassy highlands. In time, huge herds of giant four-legged animals grazed. Saber-toothed cats hunted the grazers. After millions of years, the parade of giant beasts gradually ended. Perhaps the climate became too cold. Perhaps food became scarce. Perhaps too many animals crowded certain areas. Perhaps humans hunted some mammals into extinction. Scientists are not certain why so many of the giant mammals disappeared. But by the time humans had settled much of the world, 10,000 years ago, almost all the giants were gone.

Vanished giants from the distant past make human beings look small. The artist drew all portraits to the same scale. In each chapter, you'll see small drawings in boxes like the one on the left. They'll show you how the animals in that chapter compare in size with the girl below. The creatures that appear here, and throughout the book, represent the many different kinds of animals that lived long ago.

LISA BIGANZOLI, N.G.S. STAFF

Equus caballus
Modern horse

Hyracotherium or Eohippus
Dawn horse

Homo sapiens
Adult and child

Baluchitherium
Giant hornless rhino

Gigantocamelus
Giant camel

Glyptodon
Glyptodont

Aepycamelus
Giraffe-camel

Diprotodon
Giant marsupial

Felis atrox
Giant lion

Felis leo spelaea
Cave lion

Thylacosmilus
Marsupial sabertooth

Smilodon
Saber-toothed cat

Elephas falconeri
Pygmy mammoth

Mammuthus imperator
Imperial mammoth

Mammut americanum
American mastodon

Castoroides ohioensis
Giant beaver

Megaloceros giganteus
Giant deer

Moropus
Slow-footed beast

Eremotherium
Giant ground sloth

Dinohyus
Giant pig

Brontotherium
Thunder beast

HORSES YESTERDAY AND

These horses in the San Diego Zoo are similar to horses that lived during the late Ice Age. They are

TODAY

BY CATHERINE O'NEILL

Until about 8,000 years ago, many kinds of horses ran wild across the plains of North and South America. Probably some looked much like those you see on farms today. Then all the American horses disappeared. After a long absence, the horse came back. Soldiers and explorers brought horses from Europe on their ships.

Scientists aren't sure why the earlier horses died out. The climate might have changed, turning most of the plains into deserts. Perhaps horses did not have enough water and food. When they did return, they made themselves at home. Stray animals ran free. Soon huge herds of horses roamed the Great Plains. They lived where their American relatives had grazed thousands of years earlier. They became part of American history. Indians captured, tamed, and rode them. Cowboys considered them equal partners on long cattle drives.

Ancient horses, small as this tiny mare (above), hardly looked like horses. During millions of years, their descendants became bigger and more horselike. Miniature horses today are true horses bred down in size by humans.

Przewalski (per-zhih-VAHL-skee) horses.

25

WHERE SMALL IS BIG

People have always liked small things. In Europe, kings and queens often kept small horses as pets for their children. Today many breeders in the United States raise miniature horses as a hobby or as a business. Some started when mini-horses were imported during the 1940s from England and The Netherlands. Breeders there had mated small horses with other small horses or with ponies. Then they mated the young to produce smaller and smaller animals with each generation.

One American breeder of miniature horses is Bob Pauley, of Hobby Horse Farm, at Bedford, Virginia. He and his family care for about 250 of the smallest horses in the world. The Pauleys own small stallions and little mares and lots of young, toy-size horses just trying out their legs. One thing the Pauleys do not have is a collection of large horses. The farm's biggest horses are only 34 inches tall (86 cm) at the withers, the ridge above the shoulder bones.

Taking care of 250 horses, no matter how small they are, is a big job. The Pauley children—Robert, 15, Tammy, 11, and Mark, 6—help out. Each day, one walks through the fields to check the horses. The children also help feed, groom, exercise, and train the horses for shows. Miniature horse shows differ from most other horse shows. No one—not even a child—rides the horses. Instead, the horses compete for awards on the basis of how they look and how they behave.

Small boy meets smaller horse (left). Mark Pauley, 6, of Bedford, Virginia, pets week-old Cricket. Mark's father breeds horses that at birth may be only 15 inches tall (38 cm), a bit taller than their full-grown ancestors of 55 million years ago.

"You want to make him smooth," Tammy Pauley, 11, says as she grooms Toy Boy. Good care and feeding brought a blue ribbon to this little stallion in a 1979 national horse show.

BIRD'S-EYE VIEW

At the dawning of the Age of Mammals, a small horselike animal lived in North America. It was only a foot tall, about the size of a fox terrier. It was so small that one of its enemies might have been a giant bird (right). The little horselike mammal had four toes on its wide front feet and three toes on its back feet. It padded along the soft ground. North America was warmer then. Forests covered most of the land. Grass was just beginning to appear. The little animal ate leaves from shrubs and small trees. It had a short snout shaped somewhat like that of a dog.

Some scientists call this first known horselike animal *Hyracotherium* (hy-rack-uh-THIH-ree-um). Others call it *Eohippus* (ee-uh-HIP-us) which means "dawn horse." Herds of *Eohippus* probably browsed on gentle slopes where the Rocky Mountains were beginning to rise.

Fossils of this horse have been found in the Rockies and in many other places. The fossils help scientists picture how *Eohippus* looked. The painting on these pages shows an *Eohippus* herd running from a big bird 55 million years ago. Over many millions of years, the ancient horses gradually changed, becoming larger and more like the horses of today.

The huge, feathered creature in the painting gradually died out. It was a giant bird called *Diatryma* (die-uh-TRY-muh). It stood 7 feet tall (2 m). People have nicknamed it "terror bird." Some scientists think the terror bird ate mostly plants. Others believe it preyed on small animals, including *Eohippus*. In this imaginary scene, early horses flee from the terror bird. *Eohippus* could run and dodge among the scattered trees. That was probably its best defense against enemies.

Small horselike animals flee from a "terror bird." This scene might have taken place in North America 55 million years ago. Scientists aren't sure terror birds ate meat. But they do know that the huge birds and the little horses lived in the same places at the same time.

LOIS SLOAN

Under a hot Florida sun, this graduate student prepares a fragile fossil before taking it out of the ground. She is Ann Pratt, of Worcester, Massachusetts. Ann studies the earth's past at the University of Florida. Here, she has uncovered ancient horse bones. This site has yielded fossils since 1931. The horse bones are about 16 million years old. They look cracked, so Ann decides to enclose them and the surrounding dirt in a jacket. She'll cover them with tissue paper, then add bandages of wet plaster of Paris. When the plaster dries, she will use the trowel to cut under the jacket and flip it upside down. If all goes well, Ann can then safely take the bones—in their jacket—to the laboratory.

DIGGING UP THE PAST

How do people know that horses lived in North America millions of years ago? The record is there to read. But people need special knowledge and skills to read it. Scientists say that the fossil record of the horse is one of the most complete of any animal. As a result, they know more about how the horse changed through time than they know about most other living creatures. They know that by the time the Ice Age came, little *Eohippus* had changed, through many stages, to *Equus* (EK-wus), the larger horse of today.

Paleontologists work with fossil horse bones the same way they work with bones of other animals. When they find the fossils they take them to laboratories for study. Fossil study reveals many things about the past. The rock and dirt in which the fossils are found tell paleontologists what the landscape was like when an animal lived. The rocks may contain plant fossils that give even more information.

Geologists fill in other pieces of the puzzle. Geologists are scientists who study the earth and how it was formed. They often can date fossils by studying the layers of material around them. Other methods of finding the age of fossils require the use of special equipment.

These pages show a graduate student

Ann makes a map of her find (above). She sketches the bones she found and the soil around them. Using the compass, she draws an arrow pointing north.

With help from Richard Hulbert, a University of Florida graduate student, Ann measures the depth at which she found the fossils. She will add this information to her map.

31

from the University of Florida, in Gainesville. She is working at a site nearby that contains ancient horse bones. After a major find at this Thomas Farm Site more than 50 years ago, Harvard University bought the site. Later Harvard gave it to the University of Florida. Both schools use it today.

As you look at the pictures, you can see how carefully paleontologists work at the site. In the laboratory, where the students take the bones they have found, the careful work continues. The students measure the bones and prepare them for storage. They study the material in which they found the bones. They wash buckets of rock chips and dirt from the dig site through screens. This helps them recover fossils as tiny as mouse teeth. To a paleontologist, no detail is too small for attention.

Ann prepares cloth strips like the ones doctors use to set broken bones (right). She will wrap the plaster-soaked strips around the bones she found. The plaster will keep the bones from being broken on the way to the laboratory.

Ann wraps her find (left). She has already covered the fossils with tissue paper to keep the plaster from sticking to them. "To make sure the jacket is sturdy, I drape the bandages around, across, and down the length of the jacket," Ann explains. Next, she will allow the jacket to dry. On a sunny day, drying usually takes about 15 minutes.

Ann smiles with relief when the bones and their jacket come out in one piece (right). To get the package out, she cut away the earth under the jacket. Then she carefully flipped the plaster package of fossils into her hands. It will travel to the lab bottom up, like this.

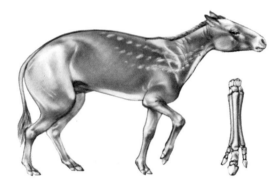

Forest-dwelling Eohippus *(ee-uh-HIP-us) stood only 12 inches tall (30 cm). It was the first known ancestor of today's horse. The small mammal (above) had four toes on its front feet and three on its back feet.* Eohippus *lived about 55 to 51 million years ago.*

An ancient horse named Mesohippus *(mez-uh-HIP-us), lived from about 38 million to 26 million years ago (left). It grazed in open areas. This horse stood about 2 feet tall (61 cm) at the shoulder. It had only three toes on its front feet. Side toes were not used in running on the hard, grass-covered land where* Mesohippus *lived. It could run faster and farther without the little side toes that* Eohippus *had. Hard running had become the horse's way of life.*

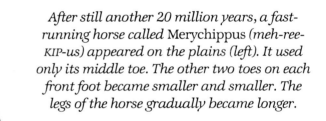

After still another 20 million years, a fast-running horse called Merychippus *(meh-ree-KIP-us) appeared on the plains (left). It used only its middle toe. The other two toes on each front foot became smaller and smaller. The legs of the horse gradually became longer.*

One of the first one-toed horses, Dinohippus *(die-nuh-HIP-us) ran especially well on hard ground (right). It stood 47 inches (119 cm) at the shoulder.* Dinohippus *lived from 11 to 2 million years ago. Many other kinds of horses lived at the same time. Scientists think some form of* Dinohippus *was the common ancestor of today's horses, zebras, and donkeys.*

HORSES THROUGH HISTORY

When *Eohippus* lived, wet, tropical forests covered the earth. The four-toed front feet of the dawn horse kept it from sinking into the soft ground of the forest. Its short teeth had bumpy surfaces well suited to grinding up the leaves it ate.

But during the next several million years, the earth changed. In North America, many forests gave way to mountains and grassy plains. Grass is tougher to chew than leaves. The plains provide few places to hide from hunting animals. The plains horse became a grazer and a runner.

These changes happened very gradually. Not all horses living on earth changed in the same ways. In general, the animals grew larger. Their legs grew longer. Their little side toes disappeared. Finally they had only one toe. This one toe became the hoof of the horses, zebras, and donkeys of today.

More complicated and bigger teeth developed for chewing coarse grasses. As the teeth changed, so did the shape of the horses' heads.

By about four million years ago, *Equus* had appeared in many parts of the world. Two million years later, slender plains horses had become 60 inches tall (152 cm). Forest horses grew heavier and several inches taller. The horse had become a giant, a successful resident of a changed world.

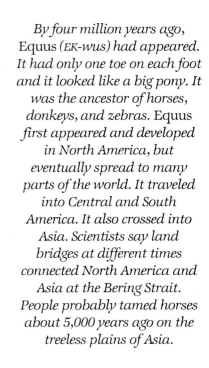

By four million years ago, Equus (EK-wus) had appeared. It had only one toe on each foot and it looked like a big pony. It was the ancestor of horses, donkeys, and zebras. Equus first appeared and developed in North America, but eventually spread to many parts of the world. It traveled into Central and South America. It also crossed into Asia. Scientists say land bridges at different times connected North America and Asia at the Bering Strait. People probably tamed horses about 5,000 years ago on the treeless plains of Asia.

HORSES OF TODAY

People have been taming horses for thousands of years. Probably the Asians did it first. About 5,000 years ago horses began helping people with their daily work.

The horse has helped human beings ever since. They have ridden it, used it in plowing and for pulling carts, taken it onto fields of battle, and loved it as a companion and pet. In many countries today, people still depend on horses to pull plows and to carry loads.

There are many different breeds of horses. Draft horses, like the huge, gentle Clydesdales, are good at pulling wagons and plows. Riding horses, like the quarter horse, are at home on cattle ranches. Race horses, like the Thoroughbred, are bred for speed, and many live busy lives on horse farms or at the racetracks. Whether they're Tennessee Walking Horses or Shetland ponies, all of today's horses have a common ancestor—*Eohippus*, the little dawn horse that lived 55 million years ago.

A young Thoroughbred tries out its legs as its mother grazes on a horse farm in Maryland (below). The Thoroughbred is one of at least 180 different breeds of horses. Most breeds were developed by humans to perform special tasks.

ANIMALS ANIMALS/JERRY COOKE

Two Shetland ponies graze on the rocky, windswept islands where the breed originated (left). The Shetland Islands lie about 200 miles (322 km) north of Scotland. Many people buy gentle Shetland ponies for their children.

The Clydesdale is a gentle giant with strong muscles (right). This stallion weighs 1,900 pounds (862 kg). He stands 17 hands high, measured from front hoof to the withers, the ridge above the shoulder bones. Breeders measure horses in "hands." One hand equals four inches (10 cm). This horse is almost as big as the giant forest horses of the Ice Age. Clydesdales descend from horses bred centuries ago to carry knights in armor into battle.

COURTESY OF ANHEUSER-BUSCH

E. HOSKING/BRUCE COLEMAN INC.

CHAPTER 3

RHINOS AND OTHER

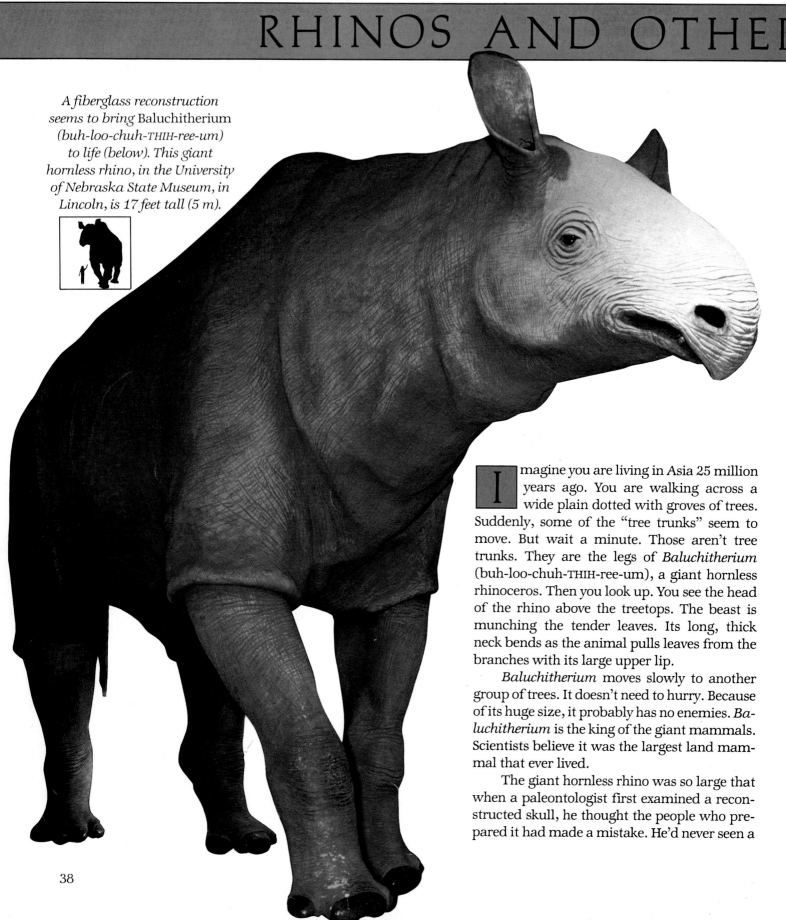

A fiberglass reconstruction seems to bring Baluchitherium (buh-loo-chuh-THIH-ree-um) to life (below). This giant hornless rhino, in the University of Nebraska State Museum, in Lincoln, is 17 feet tall (5 m).

Imagine you are living in Asia 25 million years ago. You are walking across a wide plain dotted with groves of trees. Suddenly, some of the "tree trunks" seem to move. But wait a minute. Those aren't tree trunks. They are the legs of *Baluchitherium* (buh-loo-chuh-THIH-ree-um), a giant hornless rhinoceros. Then you look up. You see the head of the rhino above the treetops. The beast is munching the tender leaves. Its long, thick neck bends as the animal pulls leaves from the branches with its large upper lip.

Baluchitherium moves slowly to another group of trees. It doesn't need to hurry. Because of its huge size, it probably has no enemies. *Baluchitherium* is the king of the giant mammals. Scientists believe it was the largest land mammal that ever lived.

The giant hornless rhino was so large that when a paleontologist first examined a reconstructed skull, he thought the people who prepared it had made a mistake. He'd never seen a

HOOFED ANIMALS

BY JACQUELINE GESCHICKTER

Too huge to hug! Harmony Voorhies, 12, of Lincoln, Nebraska, can barely get her arms halfway around one of Baluchitherium's *knees (right). This lifelike reconstruction has legs as thick as tree trunks. The living animal needed enormous legs to support its heavy body.*

The white rhino of Africa (below, left) is second in size only to the elephant among land mammals living today. Yet, next to its ancient relative, Baluchitherium *(below), today's white rhino looks like a toy model.*

LOIS SLOAN

mammal skull so large. It measured more than 4 feet (1 m) from front to back. Later, scientists put together an entire skeleton. They found that the animal stood about 18 feet tall (5 m) at the shoulder, nearly as high as a two-story house. Scientists discovered the bones in Baluchistan, a region in southwest Asia. They named the animal *Baluchitherium*, which means "beast of Baluchistan."

These giant hornless rhinos may have wandered in herds across the wooded plains of Asia. Large numbers of their smaller rhino relatives lived in Asia and on other continents.

39

Thunder beasts come to a pool to drink. For almost 20 million years, such huge rhinoceros-like animals as these wandered the plains of North America, Asia, and Europe. No one knows why they all died out about 25 million years ago. No descendants live today.

LLOYD K. TOWNSEND

THUNDER BEASTS

A century ago, rains in the badlands of the area that is now South Dakota and Nebraska washed huge bones out of the earth. The Plains Indians believed these bones came from giants. Railroad men laying tracks across North America came upon the bones. Soldiers also found them.

Stories about these giant bones reached Professor Othniel C. Marsh of Yale University. In the 1870s, Professor Marsh and some of his students journeyed into Sioux Indian lands to look for fossils. A major find was the remains of a gigantic beast, a beast whose movement in herds across the plains could have sounded like thunder. Professor Marsh named his discovery *Brontotherium* (brahn-tuh-THIH-ree-um). The name means "thunder beast."

Marsh and the Sioux Indians became good friends. The Indians called Marsh the "Big Bone Chief." They allowed him to continue hunting bones on their lands.

The rugged, empty badlands region of today looked quite different when *Brontotherium* lived there 35 million years ago. Then, herds of small three-toed horses roamed grassy plains. Humpless camels fed on the leaves of trees. Wolflike animals and saber-toothed cats prowled in search of prey.

Brontotherium, a distant relative of today's rhinoceros, measured 8 feet tall (2 m) at the shoulder. It was about the size of today's Asian elephant.

Instead of having a pointed horn on its snout, as a rhino does, the thunder beast had a Y-shaped horn. Scientists believe the horn served one main purpose: fighting rivals for mates. They found skeletons with ribs that had been broken, possibly during such fights. The ribs had healed while the thunder beasts were still alive.

BALUCHITHERIUM

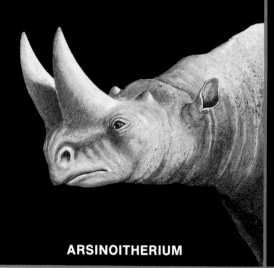

ARSINOITHERIUM

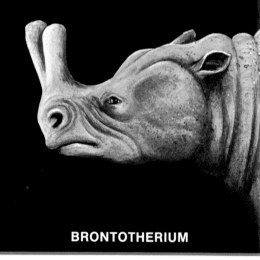

BRONTOTHERIUM

FROM HEAD TO TOE

Giants from the past had many kinds of heads and hooves. Each foot at the bottom of these pages belonged to the animal whose head is directly above it. Baluchitherium *lived in Asia 25 million years ago.* Arsinoitherium *(ar-suh-noy-THIH-ree-um) could be found in Africa about 35 million years ago. At about the same time,* Brontotherium *(brahn-tuh-THIH-ree-um) and* Uintatherium *(yoo-in-tuh-THIH-ree-um) roamed the plains of North America. These four beasts look a little like rhinos. But only* Baluchitherium *is a member of the rhino family.* Moropus *(MAWR-uh-pus), with a head like a horse, lived in North America about 25 million years ago.* Aepycamelus *(ee-pea-kuh-ME-lus), a member of the camel family, trotted across the plains of North America about ten million years ago.*

The heads and feet in this prehistoric picture-show make it clear why the Age of Mammals is known as a time of natural experimentation. Animals need special features to help them survive competition and adjust to changing surroundings.

Each foot pictured below belonged to the animal whose head is directly above it. *Baluchitherium* and the three animals next to it needed big feet and thick, heavy legs to support their enormous bodies. But big-footed beasts often were clumsy and slow. These animals could not outrun their enemies.

Baluchitherium was so big it probably did not have to defend itself. It was the largest known land mammal that ever lived. *Arsinoitherium* (ar-suh-noy-THIH-ree-um), *Brontotherium*, and *Uintatherium* (yoo-in-tuh-THIH-ree-um) were somewhat smaller. These animals could defend themselves with their

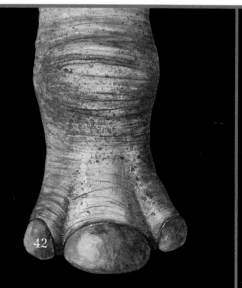

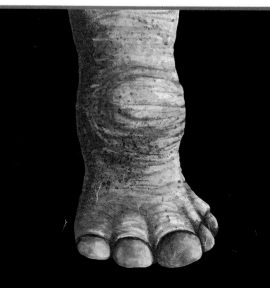

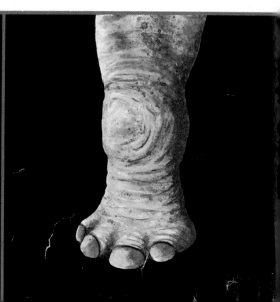

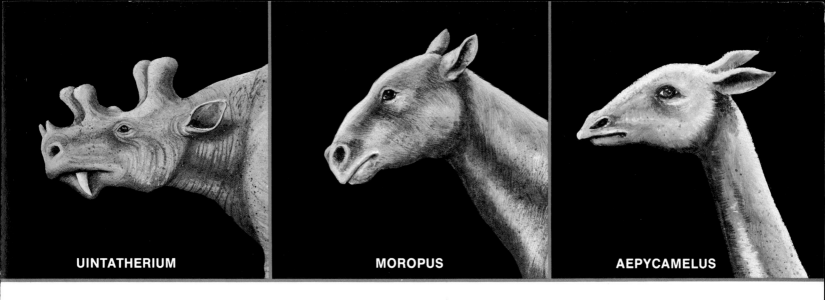

UINTATHERIUM **MOROPUS** **AEPYCAMELUS**

horns. Two large, pointed horns grew on the snout of *Arsinoitherium*. Two smaller horns stuck out from its forehead. *Brontotherium* could battle rivals with its Y-shaped horn.

Uintatherium had six horns on its head. Two daggerlike canine teeth grew down from its upper jaw. These teeth looked a little like those of a saber-toothed cat.

Moropus (MAWR-uh-pus) had a catlike feature, too. Long claws grew on its toes. Most animals with claws use them to catch and hold prey. Some experts think *Moropus* used its claws to hold tree branches while it was eating the leaves. The head of *Moropus* looked like the head of a horse. This combination of claws and a horselike head is unusual.

Aepycamelus (ee-pea-kuh-ME-lus) had no trouble getting a meal from the treetops. Its long legs and a neck like a giraffe's helped it reach high branches. Unlike the other animals

shown here, *Aepycamelus* had only two toes on each foot. Like a deer or a wild horse, it could move fast on its thin legs to escape danger.

Being able to outrun or to overpower enemies did not always mean that the species would survive, however. To survive, an animal had to be well suited to the place where it lived. If its environment changed, the animal had to be able to adjust to the change, or to find a new home with a suitable environment. If it could not do either, it lost out to other animals that did adjust.

The animals on these pages did not eat different kinds of food. All of them fed only on the leaves of trees and bushes. They did not have teeth strong enough to chew dry, tough grasses. Eventually the climate changed. It became drier. Grasslands took the place of trees. When this happened, these animals lost their food supply, and they died out.

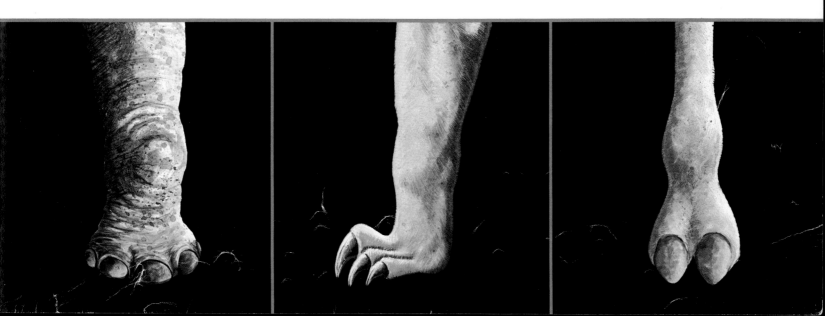

44

GRAVEYARD OF GIANTS

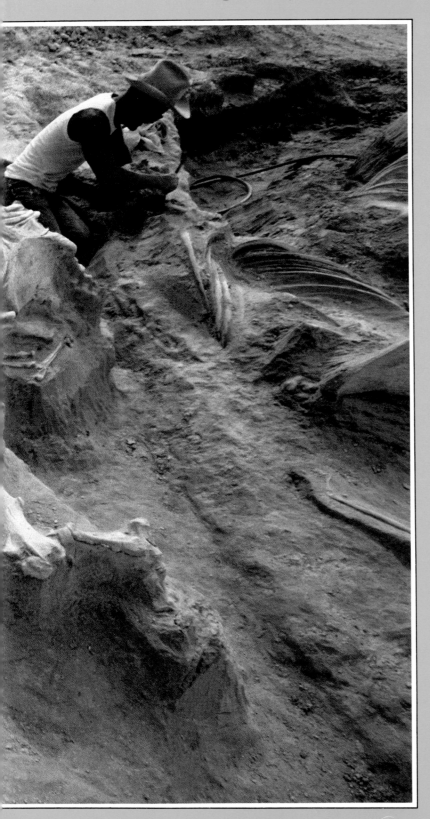

Dr. Michael R. Voorhies and associates (left) clean skeletons of Teleoceras *(tel-ee-AHS-er-us). This animal looked like a hippopotamus, but was related to rhinos. "Its stomach almost touched the ground," says Dr. Voorhies.*

In an area only about as large as a basketball court (above), paleontologists found fossils from 300 animals in northeast Nebraska.

E ach year scientists make discoveries that help solve old riddles. One animal that long baffled the experts was the rhinoceros called *Teleoceras* (tel-ee-AHS-er-us). It lived in North America about ten million years ago. No one knew whether it lived on dry plains or near water.

By a cornfield in northeast Nebraska, Dr. Michael R. Voorhies, a paleontologist at the University of Nebraska State Museum, found some answers. Dr. Voorhies and his team dug down through 15 feet (5 m) of earth.

The searchers found evidence that, millions of years ago, camels, three-toed horses, and rhinos often came to drink at a water hole. One day disaster struck. A cloud of ash from a faraway volcano darkened the sky. Blinded by falling ash, the animals stumbled to the water hole. As their lungs slowly filled with ash, they suffocated. Gradually the ash filled the water hole, turning it into an animal graveyard.

There Dr. Voorhies and his team found about a hundred skeletons of *Teleoceras*. The skeletons show that the rhino had the short legs and large chest of a water animal. "The animal was shaped like a hippopotamus," says Dr. Voorhies. "The water would have supported it. *Teleoceras* probably spent a lot of time soaking to keep cool, just as hippos do today."

Before he removes the fossils from the ground, Dr. Voorhies sketches their positions (above). The sketch shows that Teleoceras *babies were right next to adults when ash from a volcanic eruption killed them. Studies in the lab revealed that these animals were mothers and young. "We learned that there were 6 adult males and 50 adult females in the group," Dr. Voorhies says. "The males must have been leaders of herds of females.* Teleoceras *apparently was not a loner, as modern rhinos are."*

Finding buried treasure makes Dr. Voorhies smile (left). He and his team found dozens of fossils of horses, camels, birds, and rhinos in this Nebraska field. They covered each fossil with a plaster jacket, as shown here. Later they opened the jackets for laboratory study. "Sometimes we find unexpected things," Dr. Voorhies says. "We thought one jacket contained only the back part of a baby rhino. But under the rhino we found a foxlike fossil."

A funny face decorates the plaster jacket that protects a fossil of a young rhino (above). Volcanic ash killed the animal and covered it. This ash protected the fragile fossil until it was found. Two summers of work at this site produced 2,000 plaster-jacketed fossils.

MYSTERIOUS MOROPUS

I t took scientists an extra-long time to piece together the bones of an ancient animal named *Moropus*. For about 50 years, they thought they were finding the fossil parts of two different kinds of animals. "The claws kept showing up at one site, and the teeth would turn up at another. No one realized the fossils belonged to the same animal," explains Dr. Margery C. Coombs, a professor at the University of Massachusetts. Not until a complete skeleton was discovered in the late 1800s did scientists connect the pieces. They then named the beast *Moropus*, meaning "slow foot."

The scientists had been confused because *Moropus* had a head like a horse and claws like a cat. In spite of its claws, *Moropus* was distantly related to horses.

Moropus fed on leaves. Why, then, did it have claws like a cat? It might have used the claws to defend itself against bears and bear-like dogs. But scientists think the claws had another, more important, use. Dr. Coombs thinks *Moropus* grabbed and held branches with its claws. Then it reached up with its mouth, bit off the leaves, and ate them.

Like a giraffe, *Moropus* had back legs that were shorter than its front legs. "The back legs bore more of the animal's weight," explains Dr. Coombs. *Moropus* probably stood on its back legs while it was feeding.

Meet Moropus. *This skeleton (left) measures 9 feet tall (3 m) at the shoulder. Long front legs and a long neck helped the animal reach leaves high in the trees.*

A close-up of a front foot of Moropus *shows three claws (right). The animal's name means "slow foot."* Moropus *could pull in its claws only partway. When walking and running, it bent its toes upward. Otherwise, it might have stumbled.*

Huge Moropus *could feed with little fear of enemies. Here, it nibbles leaves. The mammal had no horns or antlers to get caught in trees. It lived mostly in parts of North America from about 25 million to about 10 million years ago. Squirrels look for food among the rocks.*

Aepycamelus *roamed the grasslands of North America ten million years ago. If there had been houses then, this kind of camel could have looked into a second-story window. People call* Aepycamelus *the giraffe-camel. It is related only to camels—not to giraffes. It probably drank the way giraffes do, by spreading its front legs and stretching its neck down.*

LLOYD K. TOWNSEND

GIANT CAMELS

While digging in Nebraska, Dr. Michael R. Voorhies found the bones of a camel almost as tall as a giraffe. It is called *Aepycamelus*. "It would have stood at least 12 feet tall (4 m)," Dr. Voorhies says. "It was spectacular!" *Aepycamelus* roamed the plains of North America ten million years ago. It was one of several kinds of camels that lived in North America at that time. Members of the camel family live today in Africa and Asia, and also in South America.

Another ancient camel is called *Gigantocamelus* (jye-gan-tuh-kuh-ME-lus). It ate tough plants, as today's camels do. It did not chew its food completely before swallowing it. After eating, the animal brought up the partly digested food, called a cud. It chewed the cud thoroughly, then swallowed it.

Today's African and Asian camels have humps. About three million years ago, some camels migrated to Asia from North America by crossing the Bering land bridge. These camels moved into dry areas of Asia and North Africa where food was scarce. Over thousands of years, they developed humps that stored fat. The fat fed them when they had no food.

Other camels traveled from North America across the Panamanian land bridge. Their descendants have no humps. Llamas (LAHM-uhs) are the best known American camels.

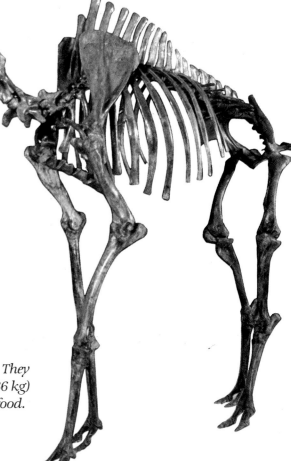

A skeleton (below) of Gigantocamelus *(jye-gan-tuh-kuh-ME-lus) stands 10 feet tall (3 m). It has long, sharp eyeteeth. The animal used the teeth as weapons against enemies, such as rival male camels. Some of these animals grew twice as tall as present-day camels.*

Bactrian (BACK-tree-un) camels live today in parts of Asia. They have two humps. Their humps contain up to 80 pounds (36 kg) of fat. The animals live on the fat when they cannot find food. One-humped camels are called Arabian camels.

THE GIANT PIGS

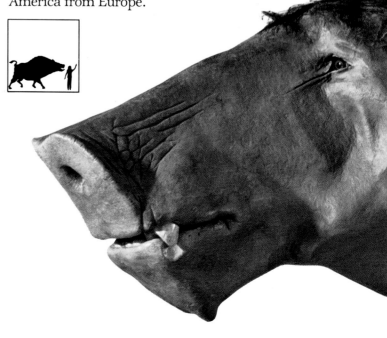

The prehistoric piglike animals on these pages grew as big as cows. They lived in North America and Asia between 40 million and 15 million years ago. "They were not the cuddly, three-little-pigs kind of animal you see today," says Dr. Michael R. Voorhies. "They had big heads and long legs, and they were not really pigs."

They looked so much like pigs, however, that the name for one of them is *Dinohyus* (die-nuh-HIGH-us). This means "powerful pig." *Dinohyus* could run fast, but did not depend on speed to attack its prey. In fact, it probably ate the meat of dead animals, rather than killing live prey. It also ate nuts and fruit. "It probably used its long legs to get from one feeding spot to another," says Dr. Voorhies. "It had to cover a lot of ground.

"The large head of *Dinohyus* and its relatives contained a good-size brain. The powerful pig was not as clever as a monkey, but its brain was good enough to keep it going for 25 million years. *Dinohyus* was the last and largest of the giant pigs." Today's pigs, even the wild boars of Europe and Asia, are only distantly related to the early giants. Wild boars found in scattered places in the United States are descended from animals brought to North America from Europe.

LOIS SLOAN

Dinohyus *(die-nuh-HIGH-us) measured 6 feet (2 m) at the shoulder (above, left). It lived 25 million years ago. It grew more than twice the size of one of its distant relatives, the wild boar (above, right). This wild boar lives in Europe today.*

One male Archaeotherium (ar-kee-uh-THIH-ree-um) fights a rival (right). A deerlike animal watches. Archaeotherium means "ancient beast." The animal lived 35 million years ago. It was one of the earliest and smallest of the giant pigs. It stood about 3 feet tall (1 m).

Scientists believed Dinohyus looked like this (above) when they built this reconstruction at the University of Nebraska State Museum. Now they know that Dinohyus had a much narrower snout and a hairier body.

THE GIANT DEER

Among hoofed giants, *Baluchitherium* was the biggest, *Moropus* probably the oddest, and the giant deer the most familiar looking. Giant deer lived in Europe and Asia until about 10,000 years ago. The largest was the Irish deer. Its name comes from the country where many skeletons were recovered.

Enormous antlers crowned the head of the Irish deer. They sometimes measured as much as 12 feet (4 m) from tip to tip. The deer's antlers were much wider than the animal was tall.

Paleontologists wondered what the rest of the animal looked like. "We now have found cave paintings that show it was a short-necked animal with a hump on its shoulders," says Dr. Valerius Geist, a professor at the University of Calgary, in Canada. Long hair covered the hump. Dr. Geist believes the hump was just for show and helped attract a mate.

Early hunters painted pictures of giant deer on walls and ceilings of caves. They may have thought this would bring luck in the hunt.

Enormous antlers top off the skeleton of a giant Irish deer (right). It is on exhibit at the Field Museum of Natural History. Scientists believe this giant deer used its large antlers to attract a mate. "It also used them as weapons in combat," says Dr. Valerius Geist of the University of Calgary, in Canada. "The big neck bones tell us that these animals probably wrestled and butted heads in contests over mates."

A male moose grazes in Alaska (below). "The Irish deer was about the size of a large Alaskan moose," says Dr. Geist. The moose is the largest living member of the deer family. A male measures 7 feet (2 m) at the shoulder.

Powerful neck and shoulder muscles help the Irish deer bear the weight of its huge antlers. Many antlers weighed as much as 90 pounds (41 kg). The more grass the animal ate, the bigger its antlers grew. Each winter the antlers dropped off. New ones began growing each spring. Irish deer got along best during warm periods of the Ice Age.

ROBERT E. HYNES

CHAPTER 4

EARLY ELEPHANTS

BY BRUCE LEWENSTEIN

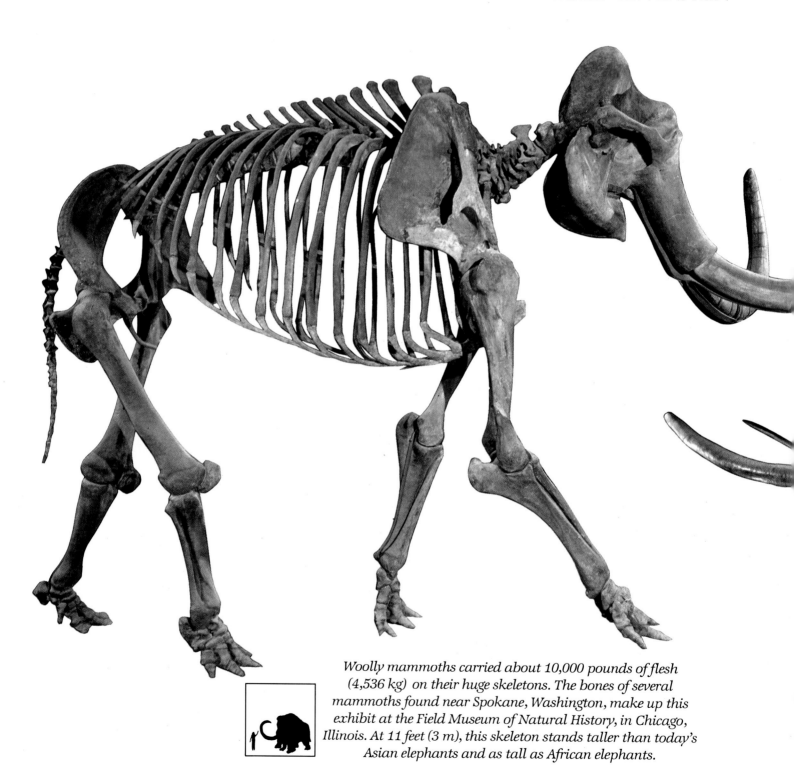

Woolly mammoths carried about 10,000 pounds of flesh (4,536 kg) on their huge skeletons. The bones of several mammoths found near Spokane, Washington, make up this exhibit at the Field Museum of Natural History, in Chicago, Illinois. At 11 feet (3 m), this skeleton stands taller than today's Asian elephants and as tall as African elephants.

The very earliest elephant-like animals known to scientists lived perhaps 40 million years ago. At that time, these animals were only a little larger than today's St. Bernard dogs. But over millions of years, they grew to giant size. A hundred or more different kinds developed.

By the time the Ice Age began, two or three million years ago, only a few kinds of elephant-like animals remained. The largest were the mammoths. Some mammoths stood more than 14 feet tall (4 m). Mastodons were a bit smaller. They reached 10 feet in height (3 m). Both animals survived the freezing winters of northern North America, Europe, and Asia.

At first glance, the skeletons of a mammoth and of a mastodon look similar. Both have long ivory tusks. Both have leg bones as thick as large tree branches.

But you will notice on these pages that the tusks of the mammoth curve up and back. Its skull is higher and narrower than the mastodon's. The mammoth's lower jaw is so short that you hardly notice it. Today's African and Asian elephants are more closely related to the mammoth than to the mastodon.

By looking at skeletons, you can't see one thing all these elephant-like animals have in common—a trunk. The trunk is really a long nose, called a proboscis (pruh-BAHS-us).

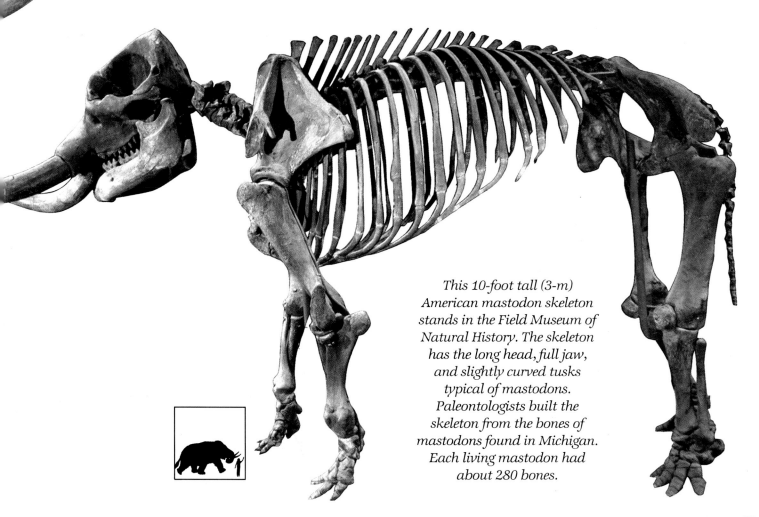

This 10-foot tall (3-m) American mastodon skeleton stands in the Field Museum of Natural History. The skeleton has the long head, full jaw, and slightly curved tusks typical of mastodons. Paleontologists built the skeleton from the bones of mastodons found in Michigan. Each living mastodon had about 280 bones.

SOMETHING TO CHEW ON

Teeth tell scientists many things about what ancient animals ate and where they lived. For example, mammoths and mastodons have completely different kinds of teeth. From the teeth and from many other clues, scientists have discovered that mammoths lived on grassy or frozen plains. Although mastodons sometimes joined the mammoths on the plains, scientists believe that mastodons usually lived in forested areas and open woodlands.

Mammoth teeth were made up of large, thin plates of hard enamel. The enamel wrapped around a softer material, called dentin. Another material, called cement, separated the plates. As the softer materials wore away, the hard enamel stood out as ridges. Scientists say these teeth worked best on prairie grass and herbs. These plants often contained hard minerals. Strong jaw muscles helped the mammoth grind the grass into pulp.

The hard grass wore the teeth down. As the teeth wore away, mammoths grew new teeth to replace them. At any one time, an adult mammoth chewed mostly with four teeth—two in each jaw. The new chewing teeth formed near the back of the jaw and moved forward when needed. A mammoth replaced each tooth five times in a normal lifetime.

Mastodons lived in areas having less grass and more trees than the areas where mammoths lived. Mastodons used their trunks to reach for leaves, and to gather bark and twigs. Before swallowing their food, mastodons crushed it between their teeth by chewing it the same way you do when you take a bite of food. Mastodon teeth had many large, rounded bumps on them. The name "mastodon" comes from two Greek words that describe the bumpy shape of the teeth. The bumps helped the teeth crush twigs and bark into food that could be swallowed. An enamel chewing surface covered the softer dentin that made up the bulk of the tooth.

Mastodon teeth did not keep growing for as long a time as mammoth teeth did. In its lifetime a mammoth had a lot more tooth that it could wear away. This allowed it to eat hard grass. Chewing grass wears teeth down faster than chewing twigs and leaves.

Despite these differences in teeth, mammoths and mastodons were similar in many ways. Both had long trunks with many muscles to control them. Like most early elephants, mammoths and mastodons used their trunks to smell and to squirt water into their mouths. Woolly mammoths even had a small fingerlike point at the tip, as today's Asian elephants do.

Both mammoths and mastodons had long tusks. Small pieces of enamel at the tips disappeared when the animals became adults. Mammoths and some mastodons had only upper tusks, but some kinds of early elephants also had lower tusks.

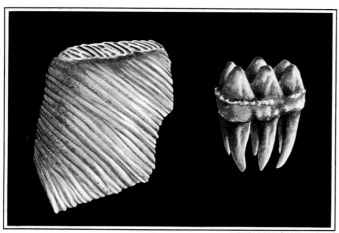

BARBARA GIBSON (ABOVE AND RIGHT)

Teeth tell the story. Hard ridges mark the top of the mammoth tooth (above, left). The ridges helped the mammoth grind up the hard grass that it usually ate. The other tooth belonged to a mastodon (above, right). Large bumps on this tooth helped the mastodon crush the leaves and bark that it ate.

The imperial mammoth, right, stands taller than the American mastodon, left. The tusks of older mammoths often grew so long that they crossed at the tips. Mastodon tusks usually curved less than mammoth tusks. Many early elephants may have used their tusks for defense. Experts believe early elephants also used their tusks to clear away snow that covered their food.

CLASH OF TITANS

In 1962, paleontologists found and dug up the bones of two mammoths near Crawford, Nebraska. The tusks of the animals were locked together. This made people think that maybe the giants had died that way 12,000 years ago.

It may have been a gray day on the North American plains. Two young mammoths began to fight. Perhaps they were fighting over a mate. Rain had turned the dusty land into slippery mud. Over and over, the two mammoths charged. They stabbed each other with their tusks. They tried to knock each other down. Suddenly, as both lunged forward, their tusks locked together.

One animal twisted one way; the other twisted in the opposite direction. Their long, curving tusks remained tangled. They struggled on the slick mud. Finally, they fell to the ground together. Wounded and tired, the mammoths couldn't lift themselves to their feet. At last, they died where they had fallen.

Paleontologist Michael R. Voorhies, kneeling, of the University of Nebraska State Museum, measures a leg bone from one of the mammoths that died with tusks interlocked. Assistants Gregory Brown, left, and Kevin Seevers put a jawbone in place. Joshua Kaufman keeps a record.

BARBARA GIBSON

Two young mammoths charge, locking their tusks together. They will slip in the mud and fall. Scientists think the tired mammoths couldn't get up because of their tangled tusks. When the skeletons were found, they still faced each other, locked tightly together.

Heather Graham, 10, with the dark hair, and her friend Laura Olsen, also 10, help out at a mastodon dig near Barnhart, Missouri. People have found mastodon bones in the area for more than a century. Heather's father, Dr. Russell W. Graham, directs the dig. He is with the Illinois State Museum, in Springfield, Illinois. He and co-worker Mike Held put a plaster jacket on a mastodon jawbone. Heather and Laura spread the plaster onto strips of cloth. "The plaster was kind of mushy, like oatmeal," said Laura. The plaster coat, when dried, will protect the fragile fossil while the scientists move it to the museum for study.

CREEK-BED BONEYARD

Sometimes people other than scientists find fossils. In 1976, a passerby noticed huge bones sticking out of the ground near Barnhart, Missouri. Soon a group of friends called the Barnhart Volunteers began to dig at that spot. They found so many bones that in 1979 they asked for help from the Illinois State Museum, at Springfield. Dr. Russell W. Graham answered the call. He identified many of the bones as mastodon bones.

"The volunteers were extraordinary in their efforts," according to Graham. With their help, he was able to discover what had made so many different bones collect in one place.

Imagine the scene 20,000 years ago. A small creek flowed toward the Mississippi River. Like other creeks, it carried bones of some of the animals that had died along its banks. Dirt and large blocks of stone fell from a bluff and dammed the creek. The bones piled up against the natural dam. More dirt settled, gradually covering the bones. Thousands of years later, the path of the creek moved, leaving the bones buried. Modern-day workers moving earth to build a parking lot uncovered them.

A mastodon gets its teeth cleaned as a bright butterfly rests on the fossil jawbone. Later, workers will put a plaster jacket on the jawbone and take it to the museum.

Heather learns from her father, right, and his co-worker Bill Stone as they unwrap the mastodon jawbone at the Illinois State Museum. Stone uses a small brush to clean dirt from the teeth. Next, he will add glue and other materials to the bone to keep it in good condition. "I really enjoy fossil digs," said Heather. "I carry tools and help wrap the bones in plaster cloth." Heather has helped her father dig at the Missouri site for three summers. He says that more than 80 percent of the bones found there belong to mastodons.

Hoe-tusker's tusks curved toward the ground like two hoes (left). Most other early elephants had upper and lower tusks. The hoe-tusker migrated from place to place in Europe, Africa, and Asia about five million years ago.

The African elephant (right) roams the wilds of Africa today. The only other kind of elephant still alive is the somewhat smaller Asian elephant. People train Asian elephants to help in such heavy work as logging and to do tricks in zoos and circuses the world over.

Short-trunked shovel-tusker (left) scooped up marsh plants in Asia about 15 million years ago. It stood six feet tall (2 m). Scientists believe the shovel-tusker was related to mammoths and mastodons.

The name Palaeoloxodon (pay-lee-o-LOKS-uh-don) means "ancient elephant." This animal (right) stood 14 feet tall (4 m). It lived in southern Europe and Africa about one million years ago.

The imperial mammoth (right) was one of the largest North American Ice Age mammals. One meaning of imperial *is "of unusual size." Scientists have found this animal's bones from the Great Plains to the La Brea tar pits near the Pacific coast. This mammoth became extinct 10,000 years ago.*

HAVE TRUNK, WILL TRAVEL

Elephant-like animals, at one time or another in the distant past, moved across all the continents except Australia and Antarctica. They came in many shapes and sizes—mostly large. Some had trunks almost as long as the animals were tall. Others had trunks no longer than their jaws. Tusks varied also. Ancient elephants used their tusks as weapons for defense. They also uncovered food with them. Today's elephants use their tusks to do the same things. For reasons not entirely clear, the early elephants died out. The mammoth and the mastodon traveled their final miles about 10,000 years ago.

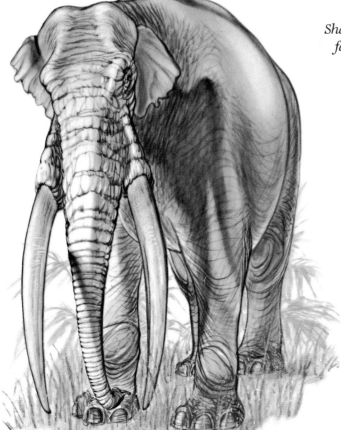

Shaggy hair kept the woolly mammoth (below) warm in the far northern areas where it lived. Its 10-foot height (3-m) made it somewhat shorter than the other mammoths.

SCIENTISTS PREPARE A NEW DISPLAY

Gary Sawyer and Richard Ferfoglia of New York City restore prehistoric fossil skeletons for museums and colleges. Sawyer is a conservator at the American Museum of Natural History. Ferfoglia owns a conservation workshop.

In 1981, Oakland Community College, near Detroit, Michigan, asked Ferfoglia and Sawyer to help them make a mastodon skeleton display. The college had found mastodon bones near the school and sent them to Ferfoglia's workshop. The New York team made replacements for missing bones. The men used a complete skeleton as a model. With plastic and plaster of Paris, they matched the real bones. They stained or painted their work to make it look exactly like the real bones. Then they sent all the pieces to the college for its display.

Mastodon bones make a strange sight on New York City's 14th Street. A passerby stops Gary Sawyer, second from right, to ask questions. Sawyer is a conservator at the American Museum of Natural History. His co-workers Richard Ferfoglia, left, and David Sundel carry a mastodon tusk and a shoulder blade to the team's workshop.

Peeling the rubber mold from a plaster cast, Ferfoglia, Sundel, and Sawyer uncover an exact copy of a mastodon tusk.

HOW TO BUILD A MASTODON

A class at Oakland Community College, in Oakland County, Michigan, measures a mastodon's leg bone (left). Class members work under the direction of Jeheskel (Hezy) Shoshani, second from the right. They measured and weighed each bone before designing the exhibit.

Diane Blakeman, 10, holds part of a mastodon skull (below). Vera Dorr, left, and Mary Kelty also help steady the skull for Wayne Cheyne. He is using an extra-long drill to make a hole for a steel rod. The rod will support the mastodon skull when all the class members later mount it for display.

Usually, museum employees put skeletons together. But when Gary Sawyer returned the mastodon bones to Oakland Community College, a class of artists, engineers, housewives, and other interested people began to build the skeleton. Jeheskel (Hezy) Shoshani, an elephant expert, taught the class. Diane Blakeman, 10, of Pontiac, Michigan, joined the class with her mother.

Class members brought individual skills to the job. Burt Knox built special drilling equipment. The class needed the equipment to drill holes through the bones to hold the steel rods that would support the skeleton.

Sister Mary VanGilder, a faculty member, supervised the painting of a scene to go behind the display. The painting shows plants and animals found in the area when the mastodon had lived in what is now southern Michigan.

Diane helped mount a leg and the ribs. "When they were drilling, I collected the dust from the bones," she said.

Later, Shoshani took the dust to Wayne

Diane, left, watches as other class members carefully hang the mastodon on a wooden frame. They are trying to find the best display position for the skeleton. Including tusks, it stretches 18 feet (5 m).

State University, in Detroit, where he continues his study of elephants. Scientists at the university are using this dust in experiments. Shoshani has put the dust into a solution and then injected it into living animals. The animals produce proteins in response to the injection. The scientists then study the proteins in the animals' blood to tell which animals might be related to the mastodon.

The class called its mastodon Elmer, because its bones had been dipped in Elmer's Glue to protect them. Class members weighed and measured the bones to compare them with the bones of other mastodons. From this comparison, they learned that Elmer was an adult mastodon. He weighed about 5,000 pounds when alive (2,268 kg), nearly the same as a large automobile. The bones in this display weighed about 800 pounds (363 kg), and the tusks weighed 50 pounds each (23 kg).

Diane looks forward to working on other projects with the class. "I just heard that I might help dig up the skeleton of a baby mastodon," she said. "I hope so!"

While Shoshani holds a back leg bone, other class members move it into final position (left). Fossil hunters did not find all of the mastodon's bones, so the class mounted only the head, backbone, and left side of the skeleton. The rest of the bones either washed away or decayed in the 10,000 years that have passed since the mastodon died.

Shoshani and class members make final adjustments (right) before adding the tusks to the mastodon's skeleton. Wires hanging from the ceiling hold the skeleton in place. Eventually, dark metal rods reaching out from the wall will support it. The skeleton stands 10 feet tall (3 m). The class worked long into the night to finish the project on time.

A MYTH EXPLAINED?

Many early elephants grew very large. When sea levels rose during warm periods of the Ice Age, some mammoths found themselves on islands, and not on the mainland. In each generation of island mammoths, the smaller individuals had a higher rate of survival. Some scientists think food was scarce on the islands. The animals needing less to eat were the ones that survived. Eventually, the smallest island mammoths stood only about three feet tall (1 m).

When people found pygmy mammoth skulls long ago, they saw a single large hole where the eyeholes of a human would be. These people could have started the centuries-old myth about a one-eyed giant named Cyclops. We know now that the eyehole of the mythical Cyclops could have been the hole where the mammoth's trunk was attached.

Phillip S. Myers, 13, of Lincoln, Nebraska, studies an adult pygmy mammoth skeleton at the University of Nebraska State Museum. This skeleton is only 34 inches tall (86 cm). Scientists found it on the island of Sicily.

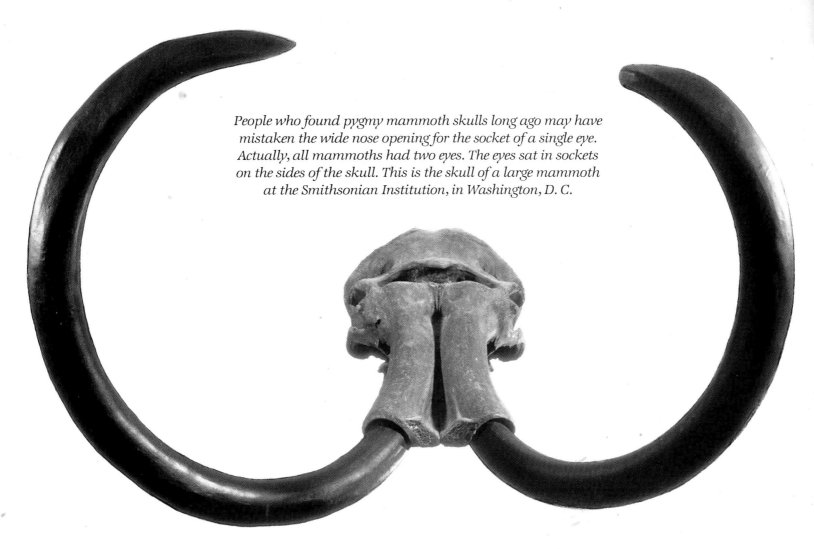

People who found pygmy mammoth skulls long ago may have mistaken the wide nose opening for the socket of a single eye. Actually, all mammoths had two eyes. The eyes sat in sockets on the sides of the skull. This is the skull of a large mammoth at the Smithsonian Institution, in Washington, D. C.

BARBARA GIBSON

Myth says that a giant one-eyed shepherd called Cyclops (left) lived on Sicily, in the Mediterranean Sea. The ancient Greek poet Homer described Cyclops as "a monstrous ogre; unlike any man who had ever baked bread, he resembled rather some shaggy peak." Today, some scientists believe that the large nose opening at the front of a mammoth skull (small picture), inspired the ancient myth.

CHAPTER 5

BIG CATS

BY JUDITH E. RINARD

You're traveling in a time machine far back into the past. You're in the western part of what is now the United States. The time: about a million years ago. Around you lie miles of grassy plains dotted with thick groves of trees.

In the distance, a herd of giant camels runs across the plains. Enormous hairy mastodons move slowly along with their young. Great shaggy animals called ground sloths tower beside trees, feeding on leaves.

In the late afternoon, many of these animals approach a stream to drink. There, hiding in the tall grass, another animal waits. That animal is a great cat. It is as big as a lion, but its front legs are larger and more powerful. Two long, pointed teeth curve down from its upper jaw. Each tooth resembles the curved blade of a kind of sword called a saber.

People call this fierce animal a saber-toothed cat. Its scientific name, *Smilodon* (SMILE-uh-don), means "knife-tooth." The cutting edge of each saber tooth is lined with tiny bumps. These bumps make notches that cut like a steak knife.

As the cat crouches to the ground, it watches the other animals. Its back legs are made for springing, not running. It does not go after fast-running animals. It waits patiently for slow-moving prey.

Soon, a ground sloth plods to the water's

This skeleton of a saber-toothed cat reveals the swordlike teeth that gave the animal its name. Scientists call this cat, and others like it, Smilodon *(SMILE-uh-don). It ranged across North and South America from about two million to about 10,000 years ago.* Smilodon *weighed as much as 600 pounds (272 kg). The cat's heavy front leg bones show that it had huge muscles and claws. Its lower jaw was hinged to swing so far open that it hung straight down, clearing the sabers for action.*

edge. As the sloth begins to drink, the cat suddenly springs. It crashes onto the sloth's back. Digging in its powerful claws, the cat pulls the sloth to the ground. Its sharp teeth stab, then rip open the sloth's soft throat. In seconds, the great sloth is dead, and the cat has a meal.

Smilodon was one of the last of many kinds of saber-toothed cats that lived long ago. Today, all saber-toothed cats are extinct. Scientists believe that the last ones died out about 10,000 years ago.

"These cats used their long teeth as specialized hunting weapons," says Dr. Larry Martin, a paleontologist at the University of Kansas. "The sabers were as long as the victims' throats were thick. The sabertooths could kill animals much larger than themselves. Many could probably pull down the smaller mastodons."

Jaws wide open, Smilodon lunges forward. This reconstruction shows what the animal probably looked like when it sprang upon its prey. The cat used its powerful front legs to knock down its victim and hold it in position for stabbing its throat. Edges of the cat's sabers cut like a steak knife. They slashed blood vessels and quickly brought death.

Closing in for the kill, saber-toothed cats attack a giant ground sloth. This exhibit is in the Denver Museum of Natural History, in Denver, Colorado. Built for strength, not for running speed, these cats could not chase down prey. Instead, they overpowered an animal with a sudden leap. Here, the sloth struggles helplessly, its foot caught in a pool of liquid tar. Such tar pools oozed and bubbled out of the earth in the far western part of North America. Animals trapped in the tar became easy targets for saber-toothed cats and other predators. Often the predators themselves became trapped in the tar.

LONG AGO IN THE WEST

It's a summer morning 20,000 years ago. The place is a valley where the city of Los Angeles, California, now stands. For weeks, the land has been dry. Hardly any rain has fallen. Creeks and even rivers have nearly dried up.

On this day, a sudden rainstorm darkens the sky. The rain pours down. Soon, a pool of water shines in the sun. Thirsty animals spot the pool and flock toward it. Many have traveled for miles searching for water.

Long-tusked mammoths arrive first at the water. They enjoy a drink, then they spray water over their bodies with their trunks. Soon, groups of long-legged, small-humped camels called *Camelops* come to drink. The camels stand together, stretching their long necks toward the water. One young camel leaves the group. It wades into the water to drink.

Suddenly, the young animal cries out. Its feet are sinking. It cannot move. No matter how it struggles, it cannot get free. The camel is trapped. This "pool" is a shallow pit of sticky tar, covered by a layer of rainwater.

The cries of the terrified animal attract the attention of meat-eating hunters and scavengers. A pack of wolves and a huge bear sniff the air and creep toward the trapped camel. Great birds wheel slowly overhead, ready to swoop down for a meal.

Before any of these animals can reach the camel, a saber-toothed cat leaps on it, bites its throat, and kills it quickly. The cat eats its fill, and turns to leave. But now, it too is trapped. Its feet are stuck in the thick tar. It cannot free itself. It will die of starvation.

Eventually, the bones of both the camel and the cat will sink into the tar, where they

will be preserved. Over thousands of years, tens of thousands of animals died in the tar pools. This tar, also called asphalt, is thick crude oil seeping and bubbling from the ground. Animals did not see the tar when it was covered by dust and leaves, or by water. The hidden tar often trapped them when they were frightened and made the mistake of running across it while fleeing danger.

In 1875, workers began to dig out the asphalt to use in road building. As they dug, they found the bones of many animals. In 1905, scientists began to explore the pits. Since then, people have found tons of animal fossils there. The area has long been known as the La Brea (lah-BRAY-uh) tar pits. The Spanish settlers in California gave the area its name. The word "brea" means "tar" in Spanish. Among the most common animal bones found in the pits are those of saber-toothed cats. Scientists continue to study the bones they have recovered. They keep learning more and more about how the ancient sabertooths looked, how they lived, and how they hunted.

Thirsty animals gather at a pool to drink. Unknown to the animals, the pool is a death trap. Underneath a sheet of rainwater lies oozing tar. This scene shows a valley in California as it might have looked 20,000 years ago. Around the pool you see, from left to right, a great bear and three wolves, horses in the distance, a mammoth and its calf, ground sloths, mastodons, camels, and saber-toothed cats. Some animals wade into the tar and get stuck. Others attack and eat the victims. Some attackers become stuck themselves. Great birds will feed on the remains.

BARBARA GIBSON

TALES TOLD BY TOOTH MARKS

The Florida State Museum, in Gainesville, displays the skull of a great cat called Felis atrox (left). The skull bears deep marks from another animal's teeth. Arrows point out the marks. Scientists believe these marks were made by another cat during a fight. Males of this species may have fought fiercely over mates. They used their sharp, pointed teeth as weapons. This cat survived this particular fight. In such fights, the animals tried only to wound, not to kill. The painting below shows how the cat might have received the wounds. Great cats like these once roamed over much of North America.

One of the most fearful animals found in the La Brea tar pits was a huge lionlike cat called *Felis atrox*. Its name means "cruel cat." It was even bigger than the fierce *Smilodon*. Some scientists think *Felis atrox* and its relatives, the cave lions of Europe and Asia, were probably the largest cats that ever lived.

Felis atrox was different from the saber-toothed cats. It was more slender, and it had longer legs. It hunted on the open plains, and it was fast enough to run down prey.

"These cats probably lived and hunted in groups as today's lions do," says Dr. Larry Martin. "The ancient cats were undoubtedly very fast. They had bodies that were perfectly suited to chasing and catching swift animals, such as horses and camels. They also hunted heavier herd animals, such as bison and musk-oxen."

For killing prey, *Felis atrox* had teeth that were shorter than *Smilodon*'s, but sharp and extremely strong. After overtaking an animal, the cat pounced on it. Then it choked the animal or broke its neck with a powerful bite. Many large cats hunt the same way today.

"*Felis atrox* was much stronger than any modern cat," says Dr. Martin, "and its bite was at least as powerful as the bite of any cat that is living today."

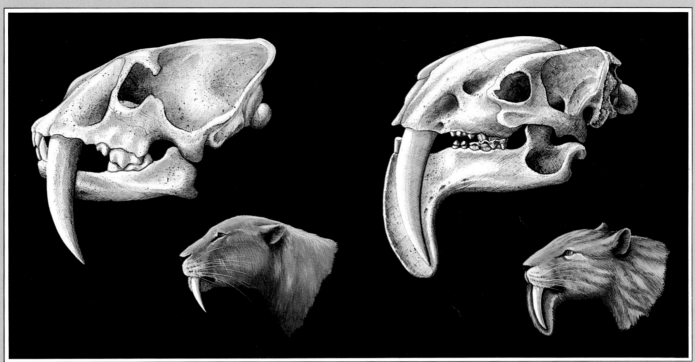

If you saw the two skulls above in a fossil bed, you might think you had found two Smilodon, or saber-toothed cat, skulls. But a scientist would see that the one on the left is Smilodon, and the one on the right is a marsupial. A marsupial is a mammal, born in an undeveloped state, that spends its early life in its mother's pouch. The heads of the animals appear below each skull. The most noticeable difference between the animals is that the marsupial has a large chinbone extending downward alongside the saber tooth. Some kinds of saber-toothed cats had similar chinbones. So scientists look at the jaw teeth and the small front teeth to find the telltale differences between Smilodon and the marsupial. Smilodon has 12 front teeth for biting. The marsupial has only two front teeth. They are blunt and in the lower jaw. They rub against the saber edges, sharpening them.

UNCOVERING CLUES

How do scientists learn about extinct animals that lived thousands and even millions of years ago? It's not an easy task. First, the animals' bones must be collected. Then they must be cleaned and carefully prepared for study.

The man working here is a fossil-cleaning expert called a preparator (prih-PAIR-uh-ter). His name is John P. Harris. He works in a laboratory at the Field Museum of Natural History, in Chicago, Illinois.

"I clean fossils after they have been dug out of the earth, so that the paleontologists can examine them," he says.

"The first thing I must do is clear away solid rock and other materials that surround the bones when they are found," says Harris. He uses tools such as delicate brushes and air scribes that shoot small streams of gritty powder to wear away rock material. "If the cleaned bones are very old and fragile, I then paint a chemical hardener on them. It fills the pores of the bones and gives them strength."

Cleaning and preparing the fossils is an operation that takes great care and many hours of work. But the effort is worth it. Fossils are clues to the past. By comparing fossil bones with those of today's animals, paleontologists learn many things about earth's history. They even find clues to what the ancient animals ate.

"The paleontologists must have complete confidence in the preparator," says Harris. "My work helps the scientists make exciting discoveries. The most rewarding thing about my job is that people in general are fascinated by fossils. They love to hear about the bones of extinct animals, and to learn what they can about the distant past."

Working gently, John P. Harris uses a tool called an air scribe to remove rock from a fossil bone. "This is the leg bone of a hippo-like animal called Coryphodon [cuh-RIF-uh-don]," says Harris. "It's about 50 million years old." Harris works at the Field Museum of Natural History, in Chicago, Illinois. Thousands of fossil bones arrive there each year from sites all over the United States. Preparing the bones for study takes great patience and care. "No two fossils are alike," Harris says. "Each one requires special preparation, depending on its age and condition."

Before and after. Two close-ups show the Coryphodon leg bone as Harris begins work on it (page 82) and after he has nearly exposed it (left). "This bone took four hours to clean," he says. "That's not especially long. Some fossils crumble easily and take much longer because you have to be so careful." Early ancestors of giant cats might have preyed on Coryphodon. "We know it was a herd animal," says Harris, "because we found its bones close to the bones of many other animals of its kind."

CAVE LIONS OF EUROPE

Ice Age cave lions lived in most parts of Europe and in the cold northern parts of Asia. They were closely related to the American lion, *Felis atrox*, and they grew as large or larger. Much of what scientists know about the European cave lion comes from caves. Its bones have been found in caves. Early people who lived in caves left behind painted pictures of the cat on the rock walls.

Paleontologists believe the cave lion hunted giant deer and giant bison, as well as smaller herd animals. Scientists think the big cat dragged its prey into caves to eat. They believe it escaped the cold in caves. They aren't sure whether the cave lion actually lived in caves.

Why these cats and other Ice Age giants became extinct still puzzles scientists. Many experts believe the animals disappeared because of changes in the climate. About 12,000 years ago, they say, one of the extreme cold periods of the Ice Age gripped the earth. The cold killed off some animals. Then, a few thousand years later, the earth became very warm. Some grassy plains became deserts. Some areas in the north became forests. Animals that lived on grass had no food, and they died. All the great cats lived by preying on grass-eating animals, so when their food supply disappeared, they died out also.

Other experts believe that human hunters, needing food of their own, killed many animals. Whatever the reasons, the ancient cats and the animals they preyed on are gone forever. Only their fossil records remain.

LOIS SLOAN

Perhaps the largest cat that ever lived was the early Ice Age cave lion (left, above). This cat was larger than the African lion of today (left, below). A thick coat of fur helped protect the cave lion from the cold. People called this animal the cave lion because they discovered its bones in caves in Europe and Asia. Cave paintings made by people long ago show that this lion had little or no mane. Nor did its tail have a tassel. The cave lion lived from about 600,000 to 10,000 years ago. Lions of all kinds were among the most widespread of the mammals; they lived in all climates.

Lions usually surprise prey with a sudden charge. This painting shows how two cave lions might have worked together to attack a horse. One cat leaps at the horse and snarls to attract its attention. The other cat crouches in a cave, ready to spring. Lions today often catch prey by hunting together.

CHAPTER 6

ARMADILLOS, SLOTHS, AND

I f you had lived in South America millions of years ago, you would have seen animals that were very different from those of today. Among the strangest of these were huge, shell-covered creatures called glyptodonts (GLIP-tuh-dahnts). They lived on vast, open grasslands.

Glyptodonts stood as tall as an average 10-year-old. Some of them measured about 10 feet long (3 m), and weighed about 2 tons (2 t). They looked like enormous turtles.

The glyptodonts were not related to turtles. Turtles are reptiles. Glyptodonts were mammals. Today's armadillos are related to glyptodonts. Armadillos live in Central and South America and in southern parts of the United States. Armadillo means "little armored one" in Spanish. Most armadillos are about one-tenth the size of the glyptodonts.

Glyptodonts were peaceful giants. They spent most of their time grazing on the grasslands. Their bony shells protected them from enemies. If enemies did attack, glyptodonts had powerful weapons. They used their heavy, bony tails as clubs.

LOIS SLOAN

The skeleton (above) of an ancient glyptodont (GLIP-tuh-dahnt) has a thick, solid shell. Bony plates grew together to form the shell. It protected the animal from predators. This species of glyptodont lived from about 2 million years ago to about 10,000 years ago. It lived mostly in South America. The drawings (left) compare the huge glyptodont in size with its modern relative, the nine-banded armadillo.

BY JUDITH E. RINARD

Tracy S. Carter, a biologist from Oklahoma State University, holds an armadillo weighing 86 pounds (39 kg). Dr. Carter went to Brazil to study these animals—the largest living armadillos. They dig burrows inside termite mounds and eat the termites. "They're strong," she says. "This one's claws caught my foot and broke several bones."

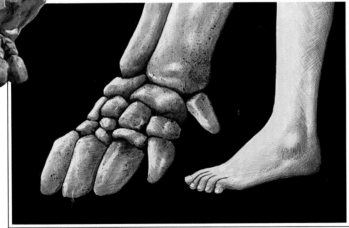

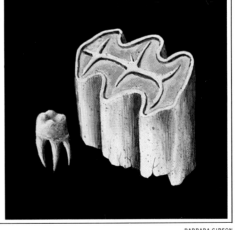

The drawings above show how a glyptodont's front foot and back tooth compare with the foot and tooth of an adult human. Glyptodonts had blunt, thick claws on their front feet. Unlike today's armadillos, which eat insects, glyptodonts ate plants. Their teeth had hard, flat top surfaces. For grinding coarse grass, these surfaces had rims and patterned ridges that looked like carvings. Glyptodont means "carved tooth."

THE TAIL OF THE GLYPTODONT

In this scene, you can see what might have happened when a hungry saber-toothed cat tried to attack a glyptodont. The kind of glyptodont pictured here grew as long as 15 feet (5 m). Its tail ended in sharp, bony spikes. The animal could swing this tail with tremendous power. Here, the saber-toothed cat lies unconscious on the ground. A blow from the glyptodont's tail knocked the cat down—and out.

ROBERT E. HYNES

GIANT GROUND SLOTHS

In the forests of South America lived enormous animals called giant ground sloths. These great fur-covered animals grew as big as elephants. They fed on tree leaves and had long hooklike claws for pulling down branches. When sloths fed, they stood on their back legs. This must have been an incredible sight. The largest sloths could reach tree branches as high as a second-story window.

Ground sloths were heavy, slow-moving animals. Saber-toothed cats preyed on them, taking advantage of their slowness. Yet the cats had to be both quick and careful in attacking a sloth. The sloth's long curving claws could be deadly weapons. Each blow could rip deep into an enemy's flesh.

Like some of the glyptodonts, many species of ground sloths migrated to North America from South America. The bones of sloths have been found in many parts of the United States. Scientists have found remains of sloths in caves in Arizona and New Mexico as well as in Chile, a country in South America. "The dry air inside all the caves had preserved some of the animals' skin and hair," says Dr. Larry Marshall, a scientist at the University of Arizona. "The hair is thick, and reddish brown in color. These remains are very important. They give us a true idea of what sloths looked like."

The sloth skeleton above is among the largest ever found. It amazes young visitors to the Field Museum of Natural History. It measures 18 feet (5 m) from snout to tail tip.

N.G.S. PHOTOGRAPHER GEORGE F. MOBLEY; BARBARA GIBSON (ART)

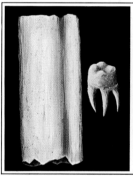

Tooth and front foot of a giant sloth make a human tooth and hand look tiny (above). The sloth had teeth well suited to chewing tree leaves and twigs. It pulled branches down with its front claws and grasped food with its tongue.

Pint-size relative of the giant sloth, a young three-toed sloth clings to a tree branch in Brazil (left). It will grow to be only 2 feet long (61 cm). Sloths spend their entire lives in trees, usually hanging upside-down. They eat at night and sleep during the day.

The largest ground sloth could reach tree leaves more than 15 feet (5 m) in the air. Here, it is looking for its usual meal. It lived in many parts of North and South America from about 2 million years ago to about 10,000 years ago. When the sloth fed, it stretched its lips and long tongue around the leaves and pulled them into its mouth—much the way a giraffe does.

ROBERT E. HYNES

ON A FOSSIL DIG

What's the most exciting way to learn about animals of the past? Ten-year-old Elizabeth Spangler and her fourth-grade classmates, of Gainesville, Florida, found that it was by searching for them.

Early one spring morning, the class went by bus to a spot near Gainesville called the McGeehee Fossil Site. There, scientists have discovered fossils of many kinds of ancient animals. Experts in paleontology from the Florida State Museum, in Gainesville, led the group.

"The best way to find fossils is to look carefully on the ground," teacher Jay Weber tells the class. "Where you see lots of pebbles and rocks, you're likely also to find fossils. Sometimes the rain washes the dirt away and helps expose the fossils."

"The dig site was way out in the country," says Elizabeth. "When we first started to explore it, I couldn't see anything that looked like bones. Then the teacher told us where to look."

The class members soon became experts at spotting pieces of bones, teeth, and shell among the pebbles. "I found some fossilized fish scales right away," says Elizabeth. "All I did was look at the ground and pick them up. They looked like potato chips."

The children also found bits of shell from extinct turtles, the teeth of ancient crocodiles and sharks, and small bones from camels and deer.

"Try to guess what kind of land this was when these animals were alive," says Weber. "There are lots of fossils from creatures like sharks and other fish. That must mean that the sea was once near here, much closer than it is today. There are also bones of land animals, such as deer. So we know there was enough vegetation to support large animals."

Fossils can give scientists

"Look what I found!" Elizabeth Spangler, 10, of Gainesville, Florida, shows teacher Jay Weber a fossil she discovered (above). "It's a fossil shark tooth," Weber tells her.

Using a scraping tool, Weber shows Elizabeth's class how to dig up pieces of an ancient turtle's shell (right). "You gently shave and brush the earth away," says Weber, a fossil expert and teacher with the Florida State Museum.

clues to what animals ate, Jay Weber tells the group. "If you find sharp teeth, you know that animal ate meat," he explained. "It used pointed teeth for holding prey and tearing flesh."

On this dig, the class found mostly small fossils. To find larger fossils, it is often necessary to dig deep in the ground.

"We don't use heavy shovels to do this," says museum teacher Lynn Shafer. "Shovels could break fragile bones. Scientists dig with small tools, sometimes as small as dental picks. They remove the dirt carefully."

"Digging and collecting fossils is only the first step in learning about them," Lynn Shafer says. The second step takes place in the museum itself. There, scientists clean and study the fossils and try to identify them. The class took part in all the steps.

"These are small crocodile teeth," museum teacher Lynn Shafer (left) tells Jonathan Stine, 10. Kelly Keller and Michael Hansen, both 10, take a look at Jonathan's find. Giant crocodiles also lived in Florida during the Ice Age.

Kevin Jensen, 11, studies a vertebra he found (above). "It's a part of the backbone of a camel," he says. Camels died out in what is now Florida at least 10,000 years ago.

VISITING THE MUSEUM

When the students returned to Gainesville, they toured the Florida State Museum with teachers Jay Weber and Lynn Shafer. There, they saw lifelike models of ancient animals on exhibit.

The students also explored a room called the Object Gallery. This room contains a collection of small animal fossils discovered in Florida. In some exhibits, visitors can touch the fossils. Instructors show them how paleontologists study fossils. In one exhibit, there are actual samples of fossil bones, clay, and sand collected from a site. Small picks and brushes that scientists regularly use to dig out and clean the fossils are part of the exhibit. Visitors can take these tools to the site to dig up some fossils themselves.

"Gently dig around the bones with the picks," Lynn Shafer tells the class. "Use the soft brushes to remove loose sand and dirt."

"This is real hard work!" says 11-year-old Kevin Jensen. "It takes a lot of patience."

At the Florida State Museum, youngsters compare fossils they have found with similar fossils on file in the museum (above). This helps them identify and date their discoveries. Here, from the left, Michael Hansen, Elizabeth Spangler, Kristine Skelley, Darrel McGeehee, and Jonathan Stine, all 10, try to match their fossils with those in collection drawers.

At The Trading Post, a member of the class leaves an object collected on the fossil dig (below). Lisa Asbell, 10, carefully adds an identification tag with her name to the bag holding her fossil. She decided to leave a piece of turtle shell she had found. "Maybe someone who didn't find one of these would like to have it," she says.

"What are these?" In The Trading Post exhibit, Lynn Shafer shows treasures in plastic bags to, from the left, Cara George, 10, Greg Crocker, 10, Michael Ferguson, 11, and Kelly Keller, 10. The bags contain rocks, shells, and other items found by museum visitors. People can choose one item to take home, leaving in its place something they discovered.

GIANT BEAVERS OF NORTH AMERICA

The beaver today lives in many parts of the United States and Canada. It is a furry animal about 3 feet long (1 m), plus another foot of wide, flat tail.

Beavers live along rivers, streams, and lakes near woodlands. They use their sharp teeth to cut down trees, and they feed on the bark. They use the branches to build dams, and homes called lodges, in the water. You may have seen beavers in zoos or in the wild.

But can you imagine a beaver almost 8 feet long (2 m), including its tail, and as heavy as a black bear? Beavers of this size once lived in North America. They existed from about 3 million years ago to about 9,000 years ago. Mostly they lived in an area south of the Great Lakes. They were not direct ancestors of today's beavers, but they belonged to the same family.

The giant beavers lived in lakes and ponds bordered by marshes. They did not eat tree bark, as today's beavers do. They fed on cattail roots and other water plants.

"The prehistoric beaver probably stayed in the water most of the time," says Dr. John Dallman, of the University of Wisconsin. "Its legs were small for its body. It couldn't move well on land with that weight."

But the giant beaver was at home in water. "Its swimming ability, combined with its size, meant that in the water the beaver probably had no enemies," says Dr. Dallman. "Even a great cat would stay away from this animal."

In a lodge with an underwater entrance, a mother beaver rests with her kits (below). The babies stay near their mother and drink her milk. Later, they will begin to nibble tree bark.

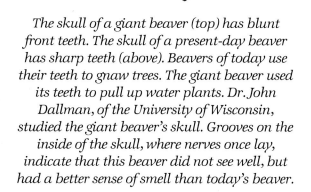

The skull of a giant beaver (top) has blunt front teeth. The skull of a present-day beaver has sharp teeth (above). Beavers of today use their teeth to gnaw trees. The giant beaver used its teeth to pull up water plants. Dr. John Dallman, of the University of Wisconsin, studied the giant beaver's skull. Grooves on the inside of the skull, where nerves once lay, indicate that this beaver did not see well, but had a better sense of smell than today's beaver.

JEN & DES BARTLETT

98

The giant beaver lived in marshland ponds of North America. It was almost 8 feet long (2 m), including the tail. It weighed about 500 pounds (227 kg). It was awkward on land, but was a good swimmer. About 9,000 years ago, scientists believe, the ponds dried up. Without water, the giant beaver died out.

LOIS SLOAN

AUSTRALIAN GIANTS

Australia today is noted for its marsupials. Ice Age Australia also was the home of many marsupials—giant ones. Marsupials are mammals with pouches. Today's marsupials include the kangaroo, the koala, and the wombat.

A giant wombat lived from about 2 million years ago to about 18,000 years ago. It was twice as long and ten times as heavy as the present-day wombat. Most wombats today are about 30 inches long (76 cm). Their average weight is about 32 pounds (15 kg).

Like wombats of today, the giant wombat ate plants—mostly grasses, tree roots, and bark. It used its powerful claws for digging. Modern wombats are also diggers. They dig deep burrows. Whether the giant wombat lived in burrows is not known.

The largest of the giant marsupials was *Diprotodon* (die-PRO-tuh-don). It was about the size of a large rhinoceros. *Diprotodon* roamed the plains in central Australia. It ate many kinds of plants.

Scientists think *Diprotodon* died out about 14,000 years ago. Human hunters may have killed it for meat.

Diprotodon was only one of the many huge Australian marsupials that vanished by the end of the Ice Age. There was a kangaroo 8 feet tall (2 m). We will never see these animals. The past hides them. Yet from discoveries by scientists, we can learn much about them.

LOIS SLOAN

KENNETH W. FINK/BRUCE COLEMAN INC.

The giant wombat (above, left) and its modern relative (above) probably looked alike except for size. The giant wombat was twice as long and ten times as heavy as today's wombat. Wombats are one of Australia's many marsupials—mammals with pouches.

Hairy-nosed wombat (left) rests near its burrow on a dry plain in Australia. This wombat has sharp front teeth, like those of the giant wombat. The modern wombat uses its teeth to eat roots, bark, and grass. Its claws help it dig a burrow. There it sleeps, keeps cool, hides from enemies, and raises its young.

Largest marsupial that ever lived was the great Diprotodon (*die-PRO-tuh-don*). The name means "two front teeth." Diprotodon *lived in Australia from about 3 million years ago to about 14,000 years ago. It was as big as today's rhino—about 10 feet long (3 m). Some scientists think Ice Age humans began hunting* Diprotodon *more than 40,000 years ago.*

LOIS SLOAN

INDEX

Composition for GIANTS FROM THE PAST by National Geographic's Photographic Services, Carl M. Shrader, Director; Lawrence F. Ludwig, Assistant Director. Printed and bound by Holladay-Tyler Printing Corp., Rockville, Md. Color separations by the Lanman-Progressive Co., Washington, D. C.; Lincoln Graphics, Inc., Cherry Hill, N.J.; NEC, Inc., Nashville, Tenn. Poster printed by McCollum Press, Inc., Rockville, Md.; *Classroom Activities Folder* produced by Mazer Corp., Dayton, Ohio.

GLOSSARY

breeds—groups of animals, usually developed by humans, that are similar in most respects

burrow—a hole dug in the ground and used by an animal as its home

environment—surroundings, including air, land, water, and living things

epoch—division of a geologic period

extinct—no longer in existence

fossil—the remains of a plant or animal that lived long ago

geologist—a scientist who studies the history of the earth and its life

grazers—animals that feed on grass

ice sheet—a glacial ice cover, especially one spreading outward over a large land area and concealing all or most surface features

mammal—any animal that breathes air, has some kind of hair, is warm-blooded, gives birth to live young, and lives on mother's milk when young

marsupial—a mammal that is born relatively underdeveloped and which spends the early part of its life in a pouch on its mother's belly

migrate—to leave one place and go to another to live

natural history—the history of the earth and the natural development of its animals and plants

paleontologist—a scientist who studies animals and plants that lived long ago

predator—an animal that hunts and kills other animals for food

prehistoric—relating to or existing in times before written history

preparator—a person who cleans and prepares fossils

prey—an animal that is hunted for food

reptiles—air-breathing, cold-blooded vertebrates—such as snakes, turtles, and lizards—that are usually covered with scales or bony plates (dinosaurs were reptiles)

species—all the animals of a certain kind (they have the same characteristics and can mate and produce young like themselves)

tassel—bushy growth of long hair at the end of an animal's tail

ADDITIONAL READING

Children's Books

Cartner, William C., *FUN WITH FOSSILS*, Kaye & Ward Limited, 1970. Cox, Barry, *PREHISTORIC ANIMALS*, Grosset & Dunlap, Inc., 1970. Fodor, R. V., *FROZEN EARTH: EXPLAINING THE ICE AGES*, Enslow Publishers, 1981. Matthews, William H. III, *THE STORY OF GLACIERS AND THE ICE AGE*, Harvey House, Inc., 1974. May, Julian, *HOW THE ANIMALS CAME TO NORTH AMERICA*, Holiday House, 1974. McCord, Anne, *THE CHILDREN'S PICTURE PREHISTORY OF PREHISTORIC MAMMALS, OUR WORLD AFTER THE DINOSAURS*, Usborne Publishing Ltd., 1977. McGowen, Tom. *DINOSAURS AND OTHER PREHISTORIC ANIMALS*, Rand McNally & Co., 1978. Modern Knowledge Library, *PREHISTORIC LIFE*, Warwick Press, 1974. Wyckoff, Jerome, *THE STORY OF GEOLOGY*, Golden Press, 1976. Zallinger, Peter, *PREHISTORIC ANIMALS*, Random House, 1978.

Adult Books

Coheleach, Guy, and Nancy A. Neff, *THE BIG CATS*, Harry N. Abrams, Inc., Publishers, New York, 1982. Colbert, Edwin Harris, *EVOLUTION OF THE VERTEBRATES*, John Wiley & Sons, 1980. Cornwall, I. W., *PREHISTORIC ANIMALS AND THEIR HUNTERS*, Frederick A. Praeger, Inc., 1968. Czerkas, Sylvia Massey and Donald F. Glut, *DINOSAURS, MAMMOTHS, AND CAVEMEN*, E. P. Dutton, Inc., 1982. Kurtén, Björn, *PLEISTOCENE MAMMALS OF EUROPE*, Weidenfeld and Nicolson, 1968. Kurtén, Björn, *THE AGE OF MAMMALS*, Columbia University Press, 1972. Kurtén, Björn, *THE ICE AGE*, G. P. Putnam's Sons, 1972. Kurtén, Björn, and Elaine Anderson, *PLEISTOCENE MAMMALS OF NORTH AMERICA*, Columbia University Press, 1980. Martin, P. S. and H. E. Wright, Jr., editors, *PLEISTOCENE EXTINCTIONS, THE SEARCH FOR A CAUSE*, Yale University Press, 1967. Romer, Alfred Sherwood, *VERTEBRATE PALEONTOLOGY*, The University of Chicago Press, 1966. Shipman, Pat, *LIFE HISTORY OF A FOSSIL*, Harvard University Press, 1981. Simpson, G. G., *SPLENDID ISOLATION: THE CURIOUS HISTORY OF SOUTH AMERICAN MAMMALS*, Yale University Press, 1980. Spinar, Z. V., *LIFE BEFORE MAN*, American Heritage Press, 1972. Willoughby, David P., *THE EMPIRE OF EQUUS*, A. S. Barnes and Co., New York, 1974.

National Geographic Books

OUR VIOLENT EARTH, 1982. *MORE FAR-OUT FACTS*, 1982. *OUR CONTINENT, A NATURAL HISTORY OF NORTH AMERICA*, 1976 (A). *DISCOVERING MAN'S PAST IN THE AMERICAS*, 1973 (A). *BOOK OF MAMMALS*, Vols. 1 and 2, 1981. (A) means adult book.

CONSULTANTS

Jessica A. Harrison, Ph.D., *Smithsonian Institution — Chief Consultant*
Glenn O. Blough, LL.D., *University of Maryland — Educational Consultant*
Lynda Ehrlich, *Montgomery County (Maryland) Public Schools — Reading Specialist*
Nicholas J. Long, Ph.D. — *Consulting Psychologist*

The Special Publications and School Services Division is grateful to the individuals and institutions named or quoted within the text and to those cited here for their generous assistance:
American Museum of Natural History: Richard Cifelli, Malcolm C. McKenna, Gary J. Sawyer, Richard H. Tedford; Jon A. Baskin, *Texas A & I University;* Kenneth E. Campbell, *Natural History Museum of Los Angeles County;* Tracy S. Carter, *Oklahoma State University;* Margery C. Coombs, *University of Massachusetts;* John E. Dallman, *University of Wisconsin — Madison; Denver Museum of Natural History:* K. Don Lindsey, Jack Murphy; Gordon Edmund, *Royal Ontario Museum, Toronto, Ontario; Field Museum of Natural History:* John P. Harris, William F. Simpson, William D. Turnbull; *Florida State Museum:* Doran Cart, Diderot Gicca, Bruce J. MacFadden, S. David Webb; Valerius Geist, *The University of Calgary, Alberta, Canada;* George C. Page Museum: William A. Akersten, George T. Jefferson; *Harvard University:* Stephen Jay Gould, Farish A. Jenkins, Jr.; Peter Houde, *Howard University; Illinois State Museum:* Russell W. Graham, Jeffrey J. Saunders; Ernest L. Lundelius, Jr., *The University of Texas at Austin;* Craig and Jan MacFarland, *Meso-american Wildlands and Watershed Program, CATIE,* Turrialba, Costa Rica; Larry G. Marshall, *The University of Arizona;* Richard E. Morlan, *National Museums of Canada;* John H. Ostrom, *Yale University;* Robert Pauley, Bedford, Virginia; Jeheskel (Hezy) Shoshani, *Elephant Interest Group, Wayne State University; Smithsonian Institution:* Nicholas Hotton III, Francis M. Hueber, Storrs L. Olson, Clayton E. Ray, Raymond T. Rye II, Henry W. Setzer; *University of Florida:* Ann Pratt, Mel Sunquist; *University of Kansas Museum of Natural History:* Deb Bennett, Larry D. Martin; *University of Maryland:* Eugenie Clark, Peter B. Stifel; *University of Nebraska State Museum:* James H. Gunnerson, Michael R. Voorhies; David P. Willoughby, Laguna Beach, California.

Library of Congress ℭℙ Data
Main entry under title:
Giants from the past.
(Books for world explorers)
Bibliography: p.
Includes index.
SUMMARY: Traces the development of the first mammals, many of which grew to giant proportions in order to survive the cold temperatures and violent changes of the Ice Age.
1. Mammals, Fossil — Juvenile literature. [1. Mammals, Fossil. 2. Extinct animals. 3. Fossils] I. Bailey, Joseph H., ill. II. National Geographic Society (U. S.) III. Series.
QE881.G48 1983   569   81-47893
ISBN 0-87044-424-7 (regular binding)
ISBN 0-87044-429-8 (library binding)

LLOYD K. TOWNSEND

Cover: In a scene from long ago, a snarling saber-toothed cat faces an imperial mammoth on the plains of what is today Nebraska. These giants lived in North America 15,000 years ago. The mammoth, a huge elephant-like creature, towered 14 feet (4 m). Its tusks were powerful weapons against enemies.

GIANTS FROM THE PAST

PUBLISHED BY
THE NATIONAL GEOGRAPHIC SOCIETY
WASHINGTON, D. C.

Gilbert M. Grosvenor, *President*
Melvin M. Payne, *Chairman of the Board*
Owen R. Anderson, *Executive Vice President*
Robert L. Breeden, *Vice President,*
Publications and Educational Media

PREPARED BY THE SPECIAL PUBLICATIONS
AND SCHOOL SERVICES DIVISION

Donald J. Crump, *Director*
Philip B. Silcott, *Associate Director*
William L. Allen, William R. Gray, *Assistant Directors*

STAFF FOR BOOKS FOR WORLD EXPLORERS
Ralph Gray, *Editor*
Pat Robbins, *Managing Editor*
Ursula Perrin Vosseler, *Art Director*

STAFF FOR GIANTS FROM THE PAST
Ralph Gray, *Managing Editor*
Carolinda Hill, *Assistant to the Editor*
Thomas B. Powell III, *Picture Editor*
Lynette R. Ruschak, *Designer*
Carolinda Hill, Tee Loftin, *Researchers*
Joan Hurst, *Editorial Assistant*
Artemis S. Lampathakis, *Illustrations Assistant*
Janet A. Dustin, Mary Jane Gore, *Art Secretaries*

STAFF FOR FAR-OUT FUN! Barbara Bricks, *Project Editor;*
Margaret McKelway, *Text Editor;* Lynette R. Ruschak,
Designer; Roz Schanzer, *Artist*

ENGRAVING, PRINTING, AND PRODUCT MANUFACTURE
Robert W. Messer, *Manager;* George V. White, *Production Manager;* Gregory Storer, *Production Project Manager;* Mark R. Dunlevy, Richard A. McClure, David V. Showers, *Assistant Production Managers;* Katherine H. Donohue, *Senior Production Assistant;* Mary A. Bennett, *Production Assistant;* Julia F. Warner, *Production Staff Assistant*

STAFF ASSISTANTS: Nancy F. Berry, Pamela A. Black, Rebecca Bittle, Nettie Burke, Mary Elizabeth Davis, Claire M. Doig, Janet A. Dustin, Rosamund Garner, Victoria D. Garrett, Jane R. Halpin, Nancy J. Harvey, Katherine R. Leitch, Virginia W. McCoy, Mary Evelyn McKinney, Cleo Petroff, Victoria I. Piscopo, Sheryl A. Prohovich, Tammy Presley, Carol A. Rocheleau, Kathleen T. Shea, Katheryn M. Slocum

MARKET RESEARCH: Mark W. Brown, Joseph S. Fowler, Carrla L. Holmes, Meg McElligott Kieffer, Susan D. Snell

INDEX: M. Kathleen Hogan

I
♡
katerina